THE LAST WOMEN

OF THE

DURHAM COALFIELD

HANNAH'S GRANDDAUGHTER

THE LAST WOMEN

OF THE

DURHAM COALFIELD

HANNAH'S GRANDDAUGHTER

MARGARET HEDLEY

FOREWORD BY HILLARY CLINTON

The History Press

First published 2024

The History Press
97 St George's Place, Cheltenham,
Gloucestershire, GL50 3QB
www.thehistorypress.co.uk

British Library Cataloguing in Publication Data.
A catalogue record for this book is available from the British Library.

ISBN 978 1 80399 419 2

Typesetting and origination by The History Press
Printed and bound in Great Britain by TJ Books Limited, Padstow, Cornwall.

MIX
Paper from
responsible sources
FSC® C013056

Trees for Life

CONTENTS

ACKNOWLEDGEMENTS

I am grateful to lots of people for sharing their knowledge about different aspects of this book. I have asked questions about what must have appeared random topics and sometimes didn't even explain why I wanted to know! But the people I asked have been amazing. I will try to mention everyone who has helped in any way at all, and I know this is dangerous as I am bound to leave someone out and for that I apologise.

George Bean, Fred Bromilow, Bill Burrell, David Jordan, Norma Mills, Keith Newton, Dorothy Peacock, Carol Reay, Joan Scott, Gordon Tempest, Tom Tunney, Denise Waite, Mary Walker, Margaret Wharrier, Wheatley Hill History Club, Wheatley Hill Mothers Club, Hilary Whitbread, Beatrice Young.

However, most of my thanks must go to my family. To my long-suffering husband, John Hedley, who has supported me through every step of this very bumpy journey and my children and grandchildren for their continued encouragement.

Family Tree of Hannah Hall

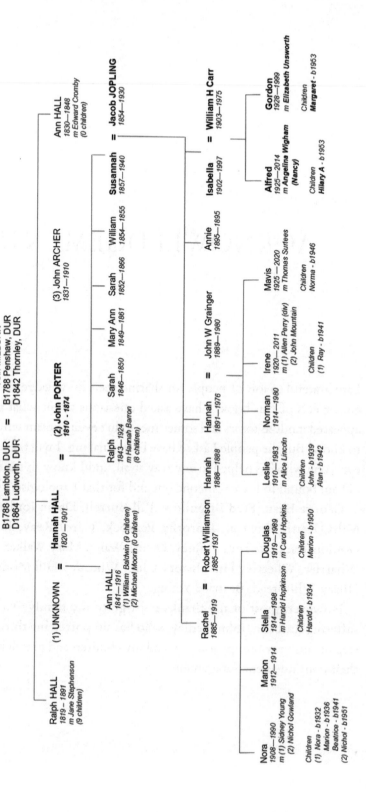

FOREWORD

I grew up hearing stories from my family members who emigrated to the United States from a County Durham mining community in the nineteenth century. My paternal grandfather, Hugh Simpson Rodham, came from England as a child with his parents and siblings to Scranton, Pennsylvania, in the 1880s. My grandmother, Hannah Jones Rodham – who went to work very young in a silk mill in Scranton, where she met Hugh – often talked about her great-grandparents who came from the small coal mining villages of southern Wales. That's what drew me to Margaret Hedley's remarkable trilogy of books about the women of the Durham coalfields.

Histories can be epic tales of wars, empires, economic forces, presidents, and kings. But I find myself most drawn to stories that illustrate the lives of ordinary people who, in their own small ways, shaped our world.

As I was reading about Margaret's great-great-grandmother Hannah Hall, I began to picture my great-great-grandmother in Hannah's place. She lived in the north of Durham while Hannah lived in the east, but I was able to imagine the type of life she and her family had lived based on Hannah's story. The circumstances of their lives would have been similar, and they would have both faced the difficult decision of staying in the only home they'd ever known or sailing into an unknown future for a chance at a better life.

Through Margaret's family saga between 1820 and 1968 – an era when life was lived around coal – we meet ordinary people caring for their families, making hard choices, and searching for meaning. The women married to coal miners were caregivers who waited at home, not with empty hands but with a relentless list of household tasks to carry out. They worried about whether their husbands would come home or if they'd join the list of miners killed in the dangerous mines. If that happened, they knew they would lose their family's only source of income and the roof over their heads.

In her latest book, *The Last Women of the Durham Coalfield*, Margaret brings her family's journey into the present with her own story. As the title suggests – and as Margaret witnessed at the age of 15 – the coal mines on which her family and their village relied closed forever. The impacts on the surrounding community were enormous. Her story shows not just how economies and industries changed, but how those changes affected the way people lived.

That's why Margaret's meticulous research and vivid prose is so critical. So often, books about County Durham tell us about the husbands, fathers, and sons who worked in the dangerous and dirty coalfields. But through their actions, daily tasks, and choices, the women at home formed the warp and weft of history. From Industrial Age hardship to post-war affluence to the women's movement, the world went through monumental changes during Margaret's family's lifetimes, and they met the changes with resilience and resourcefulness.

There was progress on so many fronts, and much of that progress would have been impossible without the women we meet in Margaret's books. They didn't live their lives expecting that their stories would be included in future books, but their stories are essential. Without them, our understanding of the past is impoverished, our history only half complete.

I hope that Margaret's books will inspire more historians to document the daily lives not just of men, who have been traditionally centred in historical narratives, but of the women living quieter but just as important lives alongside them. As this book shows, the women of the Durham coalfield played an equal role in shaping daily life and trajectories of history in the region, just as women today are building their own futures in communities around the world.

Hillary Rodham Clinton
Former First Lady, US Senator and Secretary of State.

INTRODUCTION

This is the final part of my trilogy that started with my great-great-grandmother, Hannah Hall, who moved into east Durham with her family and was there at the opening up of the coalfield when it at last became possible to drill through the magnesian limestone at Hetton Lyons pit in the early 1820s.

The importance of Hetton is described by Les Turnbull in his publication *Hidden Treasures*, published to coincide with the bi-centenary of the Hetton Lyons colliery in 2022. His words may surprise some, but we should always bear in mind that without the Hetton project, our pits in east Durham would not have been possible as early as 1822:

> There are certain special events in life, like the landing of the Apollo 11 spacecraft on the moon, which change our perception of the world in which we live. The winning of Hetton Lyons Colliery in County Durham between 1820 and 1822 was another such event. Both these giant leaps for mankind were the outcome of years of technical development often carried out despite the scepticism of the scientific establishment of the day.

I doubt if Hannah or her family realised the massive impact the opening of Hetton pit would have on the rest of the area, but it allowed the development of a coalfield previously land-locked and concealed by the magnesian limestone into a massive expansion of a whole new society that became known as east Durham, with a deep sense of community throughout the nineteenth and twentieth centuries, and Hannah came to represent the women who were married to the men who mined the coal.

I had tripped and stumbled for several years over whether to introduce Hannah into the public domain and make her story known, but I always managed to talk myself out of it. Eventually, and recognising that the story was unique and hadn't been told before, but still full of trepidation, I brought it into existence and, incredibly, it was successful.

I didn't think there would be another book. I had certainly never planned for one, but readers had become invested in Hannah and her family and were anxious to see how they fared through the better times of the early twentieth century. There was more information for this book. Hannah's youngest daughter, Susan, could read and write, and her memory was kept alive by her youngest daughter, my grandma, Bella. There wasn't the need for speculation as there had been with Hannah's situation, but I continued to include dialogue that had proved popular with most readers. The dialogue, while not accurate, gives me an opportunity to highlight what might have been said, in the words, turn of phrase and dialect of the time.

This is the format of my latest book, only this time I am not even reliant on my grandma for primary source material, as I appear in the narrative and much of the book is seen through the eyes of someone born in the mid-twentieth century who can shed light on how women married to coal miners fared during that time up until the end of the coal industry in my village, 1968, when I was 15 years old and became one of the last women of the Durham coalfield.

My own contribution to the story is not made up in any way. It is as I remember it and supported by some evidence along the way. I may have forgotten vital details or interesting snippets that people who know me will remember, but as far as I'm aware, I have researched this book as thoroughly as my previous work.

1

THE DESTINY OF WORKING-CLASS GIRLS

There was never any doubt that Bella Jopling would marry a pitman. Daughters born into coal mining families in the early 1900s were destined to marry men from that industry, and it was only in exceptional circumstances that it didn't happen. It was the expectation of families in the coal industry and always had been. In turn, coal miners liked to marry girls brought up in the mining community because they knew what to expect. The price of coal dominated their lives. Coal owners were obsessive about sending cheap coals for export and a low selling price meant they would have to make economies elsewhere, which was usually at the expense of the miner and his family. Mining families knew how much the coal sold for and realised that profits were more important to the owners than their workforce. It was just one more of the drawbacks of life in a mining village, added to poor-quality housing, a lack of interest from landlords, who were the private coal owners, low rates of pay, poor working conditions for the men and long strenuous hours for the women. In addition, a wife had to be ready and willing to support her husband at times of industrial unrest. Marrying a girl who wasn't used to the coal industry was asking for domestic trouble as far as the miners were concerned.

Bella's family had a long association with the Durham coalfield that could be traced accurately back to the early to mid-eighteenth century in the old coal areas of Ryton, Washington and Chester-le-Street, and even though there were more opportunities for girls benefitting from a compulsory education by the time they left school in 1916, most mining families would still expect their daughters to marry a coal miner. A girl's training to reach this eventual goal began from a very early age, was overseen by her mother, and covered every aspect of household management. Bella was the first of her parents' children to be born in the twentieth century – January 1902 – a time of great hope for the Durham miners, who had been exploited for generations. After years of struggle to unionise, the Durham Miners Association had been in operation since the 1870s, and although change was slow, the miners felt it was bound to be sure. The mining families of the Durham coalfield certainly believed that the twentieth century would bring about improvements to their lives, both at the pit and at home.

Bella was born and brought up in the smallest of the colliery villages belonging to the Weardale Steel, Coal and Coke Company at Ludworth, County Durham. Since the early days of its pit in the 1830s, this village had received terrible reviews for its housing, sanitary conditions (or lack of them), water provision and sewage disposal. This negativity had been a feature of life in Ludworth during the lifetime of Bella's grandparents and parents, and was much worse during her time growing up there at the turn of the twentieth century. From time to time sympathetic outsiders visited the County Durham colliery villages – William Morris in the 1880s, Sidney and Beatrice Webb in the 1920s, J.B. Priestley in the 1930s and Mark Benney in the 1940s. Despite their visits being many years apart, all described the conditions as bleak and dreadful, and while there is no record of any of them visiting Ludworth, it was not much different from other villages and much worse than most. Even at the time Bella was growing up, road and transport links to Ludworth were almost non-existent, and to visit the neighbouring village of Thornley it was necessary to walk along the railway line. Only a cart track linked the village with its other near-neighbour, Shadforth; however the people who lived there, like Bella, had a different set of values and they didn't see it as an outsider would. Bella loved being part of the village and its close-knit community where everybody knew everybody else, and didn't seem to notice the drabness of her surroundings.

Bella's parents were respectable people, brought up to follow Victorian traditions, and both had lived in Ludworth for most of their lives and were well thought of. Her granda, Will Jopling, had owned a property in North View and ran a general dealer's shop from his front room. Her great grandparents, Jack and Annie Jameson, were the licensees of the top house – the Ludworth Inn – at one time, and while this might not be seen as a mark of respectability by some people, it was a sign that they could make a success of running to business in a very small village with fierce competition from a further two public houses.

On her mother's side, Bella's grandma, Hannah wasn't talked about much, but Bella knew she had been a dressmaker and later ran a hardware shop from the front room of her privately rented house in Margaret Street, Ludworth. From what little she knew of her grandmother, it seems that she and Bella's mother had had a falling out, but Bella wasn't aware of the circumstances. She did know that her granda had gone to Australia looking for work and that her mother, Susan, was born while he was away and didn't meet him until she was 7 years old. Susan used to tell her daughters of the children her mother lost to TB and of the tough time she had while her da was away, when it was necessary for her to work on a farm and carry out dressmaking tasks in order to make ends meet while bringing up her children, but still finding the time to help with fundraising during the building of the Primitive Methodist Chapel at Ludworth. These were the parts of her mother's life that Susan was prepared to share, but she was very vague about the rest. Susan was very good at being vague. One thing that was often mentioned about Hannah, however, was her dislike of anything to do with alcohol and all it stood for in the colliery village. This was an attitude carried on by Bella's mother, Susan, and subsequently her daughters, including Bella herself.

Bella's sisters had been like little mothers to her as she was growing up, as they were 14 and 11 when she was born, and she had a very happy childhood in the small mining community where neighbours became extended family. From an early age, children in the colliery villages learned to live with death – the deaths of elderly people that they knew well, deaths caused by accidents at the pit, deaths of children from illnesses that could not be cured and accidents inside and outside the home. However, Bella's first direct experience of death in the family came in 1914 when she was 12. Her niece, Marion, the second eldest daughter of her sister Rachel, died of whooping cough. Bella was devastated. She couldn't understand why a lovely, previously healthy 2-year-old should die from a bad cough. She saw the effect it had on Rachel, her husband Bob and also on Marion's sister Nora, only 6. She never forgot little Marion's funeral at St Cuthbert's Church, Shadforth. Bella witnessed first-hand how her family supported her sister Rachel at this awful time and this was a further indicator, if she needed one, of how important family was.

Even at the time Bella started school in 1907, education for girls was still seen as unnecessary by some coal mining families, who felt their daughters' time would be better spent learning from their mothers how to run a household in readiness for marriage to a coal miner. However, the school at Ludworth was well-attended and Bella received an adequate education for a girl of her generation and class.

With the outbreak of the First World War, the small colliery village saw some of its menfolk going off to fight, and those who stayed behind in protected occupations continued to work at the pit. Whatever happened to the men always affected the women. If there was a strike at the pit, the women had to carry on feeding their families with less money and therefore less food. If a man was injured at the pit, his wife became his nurse and carer, a task taken on alongside her already heavy workload. If her man was killed at the pit, she had to find alternative accommodation within two weeks, with perhaps no money to pay her rent. So, when some men went away to fight in the war, the priorities of the women changed. A wife didn't have to work around her husband's shifts at the pit and make food and baths for him coming and going, and she received wages more regularly from the armed forces than she did from the coal owners. However, the fear for her husband's mortality was always on her mind, whether he was at the pit or fighting in a war.

The Jopling family unit joined forces in 1914 when Bella's sister Hannah became very ill after giving birth to son Norman in June that year. The illness became so bad that Hannah spent spells throughout the coming months in the Royal Victoria Infirmary at Newcastle. Bella, her mother, and sister Rachel rallied round to help Hannah's husband, Jack. They looked after the elder child, Leslie aged 4, while caring for the baby between them, and when Jack Grainger joined the Durham Light Infantry in 1915 and was therefore unable to help with childcare, the family took the extra responsibility in their stride.

Despite doing well at school, which meant that Bella could read, write and do her sums, employment for girls of her age from the colliery villages centred around the skills they learned from their mothers, which were based on homemaking and service – either housework or shop work. The training received at the hands of diligent mothers stood the girls in good stead to be effective servants in the homes of the better off. They were taught that being able to run a clean, efficient and well-ordered home was a sign of respectability and that was what the women married to coal miners were striving for. They knew that their reputation in non-coal mining areas was of dirty, slovenly people and the women in particular were always anxious to appear respectable in all its forms: running a well-ordered home, having clean, white washing hanging on the washing line, children who were decently turned out, sending the children to Sunday School, and encouraging good behaviour outside the house, including not owing anyone any money.

After leaving school it was only natural that Bella would seek employment, and after a spell working on a local farm, she went into service at a private school at Redcar during the war, not at all discouraged by the amount and variety of work she had to do.

When her sister Rachel died of the Spanish Flu just after the end of the First World War, at the beginning of 1919, Bella was recalled from her 'place' in order to support the family. She knew it was expected of her. The family needed her help, and she wouldn't think of refusing to return. Rachel died only days after giving birth to her son, Douglas.

Her eldest daughter Nora was 10½, her second daughter, Stella, just 4½ years old. Rachel's early death required extensive intervention from her mother and sisters to keep the family unit together with each one doing their bit, and between them they took on the care of baby Douglas and the two girls without complaint while supporting Rachel's husband Bob, until the children were old enough to find their own way in the world.

In 1924 Bella married coal miner Billy Carr from Wheatley Hill and her parents moved into an Aged Miners Home at Thornley. Bella was desperately sorry to leave behind the close-knit Ludworth community and took every opportunity to visit her sister Hannah, who continued to live there. Through this contact she could continue to hear news about those who had died, those like her who had moved away, and the people still living there that she grew up with and how their families were developing. Bella never forgot her roots.

Despite Billy's job being at Wheatley Hill pit, their first house, by choice, was at Thornley to be near Bella's ageing parents. It was a private rented property in Coopers Terrace. The house, like many at the time, was infested with cockroaches or black clock beetles (it is not clear which species). Bella described them as invaders of the home when there wasn't a light on and often spoke of how every surface was covered by them when the family returned home at night. These infestations had plagued the colliery houses for years and the mining families saw it as another drawback of colliery-owned housing. However, all poor-quality housing at the time suffered from similar infestations. Despite these invasions Bella made the house in Coopers Terrace comfortable thanks to her home-making skills. Her wallpapers, purchased at the store, were much admired by visitors as she made the house into a home where she gave birth to her two sons, assisted on both occasions by her mother.

While they lived at Thornley, Bella and Billy kept hens and two pigs on land rented from local farmer Mr Roper, adjacent to their house. The day-to-day nurturing of these animals was undertaken by Bella as part of her daily routine. She would feed the hens and the pigs and collect the eggs, most of which were sold at Wheatley Hill by Billy's mother, Meggie, at 2*d* an egg. It was well known that miners' wives often had a sideline to make a bit of money of their own and to eke out the family budget, and this was Bella's. Some would make mats or quilts, or pick berries in the hedgerows and make jams and chutneys to sell, anything to help them out financially if times got even harder. Bella's mother, grandmother and great grandmother were dressmakers and made a good living out of their skills for over 100 years. However, with the availability of ready-to-wear clothing at the beginning of the twentieth century, there was not much demand for this service any longer. Despite being quite capable of making her own clothes, Bella had to look elsewhere for an income stream. The egg sales and selling of the fattened pigs added to the family budget. She also made ginger beer and sold it locally at 2*d* a bottle, her regular customers being the residents of the Aged Miners Homes where her parents lived.

As a result of these schemes, which carried on outside the formal economy and careful household budgeting, the family were able to buy a motorbike and sidecar offered for sale by their next-door-neighbour, Mr Stoddart, and throughout the 1930s would have regular outings around the area. Billy would drive the bike with Bella and the two boys in the sidecar. Bella's sister Hannah and her family also bought a motorbike and sidecar, and the two families would go on these outings in convoy. They were the first of their families to have been able to travel around the region in which they lived, as a result of having access to a private means of transport.

In 1937 Billy became a deputy at Wheatley Hill pit and as a result of this supervisory role he was expected to live in the village, so the family reluctantly moved from Thornley. Their first house at Wheatley Hill was at No. 15 Wolmerhausen Street, where they stayed for two years.

Wolmerhausen Street, Wheatley Hill.

2

GOWLAND TERRACE, WHEATLEY HILL

After leaving Wolmerhausen Street, their new address was No. 3 Gowland Terrace. Billy started work at Wheatley Hill pit in 1917 aged 14, the earliest that boys could get a job as a coal miner at that time. By 1941, because of his aptitude for pit work and ability to win the respect of the men, he was working as a grade 2 overman, having moved up through the coal mining ranks of datal work, putting, coal hewing and deputy. In this role he would be a deputy to the overman and have specific statutory duties involving safety inspections, gas monitoring and supervising coal production, and become eligible for a house in Gowland Terrace, where he had quick access to the pit if the need arose.

Gowland Terrace was built during the 1870s to house the miners at the new winning, started in 1869 by the Original Hartlepool Colliery Company, owners of Thornley and Ludworth collieries. One of the directors of the company was Ralph Gowland and he lent his name to Gowland Terrace. Most of the early colliery housing was named after directors of the coal company: Ford Street, Wolmerhausen Street, Pyman Street, Gullock Street, Grainger Street, Gothay Street, Patton Street, Smith Street, Arne Street. The streets given Christian names such as Louisa Street, Maria Street, Anne Street, John Street and

Gowland Terrace, Wheatley Hill.

Elizabeth Street would be the names of the wives or children of the directors. It was a constant reminder to the miners of who they should be grateful to for having a roof over their heads.

The Gowland Terrace houses were built of red brick and of the two-up two-down variety as opposed to the majority of the neighbouring houses at the time, which were single storey and built of a cheaper building material – limestone – which was available in abundance on the north-east coast. The Gowland Terrace houses appeared for the first time on the 1881 census. This street of houses was adjacent to Office Street where the pit management lived, Gowland Terrace being intended for middle management – overmen, deputies or foremen at the pit. The houses had an enclosed backyard and a long garden at the front, amenities that the single-storey housing did not enjoy.

The street of twenty-three houses was as near to the pit as it could possibly be without being in the pit yard. No. 3 was only about 50 yards from the pit workshops and the internal railway line that saw coals being hauled between Wheatley Hill and Thornley by the colliery tankey. The noise was constant throughout the day, caused by the hammering from the blacksmith's shop, clanking of the coal trucks and the steam and hooter of the tankey as it moved them along the sidings, together with the steam from the winding engine and the sound of the pit buzzer at the end of every shift. It was a part of life for the inhabitants of the colliery houses near the pit. When the pully wheels were working, raising or lowering the cage, a fine mist of black dust appeared in the atmosphere and attached itself to washing hanging out to dry, to babies in their prams and to people minding their own business. The colliery village had smells of its own from the smoke created by household coal fires and smoke from the pit chimneys. These were the conditions that mining families lived with day in day out, conditions that they expected, didn't even consider that there was anything wrong with and probably hardly even noticed.

The back of the houses in Gowland Terrace (which was the entrance used by all residents) overlooked the new pit baths, opened in 1939, the pit workshops and the colliery office occupied a building adjacent to No. 21. The front of the houses looked over their long gardens and a range of allotments towards Gore Burn (known locally and hereafter as the beck), the private housing of Lynn Terrace and the Colliery Hotel in the distance.

There was a footpath behind the street that was accessible at both the colliery office end and the Gowland House end, which was three doors away from No. 3 and occupied by the colliery engineer, Mr Welsh, during the 1940s. At the Office Street end, the track led down a steep bank to the beck and a rickety footbridge that led through the fields and eventually to Lynn Terrace and the Colliery Hotel. The footpath at the Gowland House end was a much wider and more accessible path that led past the allotments and eventually to a footbridge over the beck.

The Weardale Steel Coal and Coke Company took over Wheatley Hill, Thornley and Ludworth Collieries in 1888 and were therefore the owners of the colliery housing. The quality of the houses remained poor, but they were better maintained by this coal company than they had been by previous coal owners. This was due in no small part to the increased involvement of local councils in setting living standards to which private landlords had to abide, even the coal owners.

Billy hired a cart to bring their belongings from Thornley to Wolmerhausen Street, but the move from Wolmerhausen Street to Gowland Terrace was carried out without a cart, but with the help of some of his brothers who were available on the day of the move. Alf, Kit, Herbert, Billy and sons Alf and Gordon were responsible for transferring household goods the short distance between the two properties. Alf and Gordon enjoyed being involved with their uncles and loved the joking that went on between the Carr brothers. Bella packed the breakables, well wrapped up in newspapers, into the sidecar so she could be sure of their safety, for while she thought a lot of Billy's brothers and was very grateful for their help, they weren't the most careful of removal men. The move took about three hours.

Bella lit the fire in the kitchen at the Gowland Terrace house early on the morning of the move and set the kettle to boil so she would have plenty of hot water to scrub the floors of the downstairs rooms, covering them with newspapers when she'd finished. Most people wouldn't have bothered to scrub the floors as they weren't bad, but it made Bella feel better that she'd put her stamp on her new house. When the first of their belongings arrived, she was able to direct the carriers to their temporary destination. All the furniture was to be stacked in the downstairs rooms or left in the enclosed back yard until she had time to scrub the two bedrooms.

'What are ye ganna de with this?' Billy's elder brother Alf asked Bella, holding her prize aspidistra out in front of him.

'It's an aspidistra,' Bella replied.

'Aye aah naa and aah think its aawful.'

'That plant might be older than you so watch what yer doing with it. It belonged to me ma and it might have even belonged to me grandma so aah intend to look after it.'

'Why where de yer want it then?'

'Put it in the sitting room, the light's good in there'.

Alf rolled his eyes as he walked away with the plant. 'Might be better on the tip,' he muttered.

Eventually the furniture was moved, and Bella went back up to Wolmerhausen Street to start and scrub the floors there before Billy handed the keys back to the colliery office. For all it was clean, she wouldn't have dreamt of not cleaning a house she was leaving. Billy was well known in Wheatley Hill and the pride in her housekeeping skills would be hurt if she felt people thought the house was in any way not up to scratch. Billy gave his brother Alf 5s (25p) to get his brothers a drink on their way home after their mornings' work and as a token of his thanks for their help.

Bella, like most miners' wives, worked at home providing a comfortable space for her husband to come home to after his eight-hour shift at the pit. However, after 1939 there was no need for a bath to be prepared for him, as was the case when both their fathers had been pitmen, as pithead baths became available at Wheatley Hill. The local newspaper reported the occasion of the opening of the baths as 'A Red Letter Day in the Village', and it certainly was for the women who would no longer be required to start heating up water for the big tin baths that stood in front of the fire, as now their husbands and sons would return home clean and leave their pit clothes in a locker at the baths. Towels and soap were available at the pit, and the towels could be purchased for home use, where they represented excellent value for money.

The pit baths were only one of the innovations that had helped the work of women married to coal miners, but soap became an issue when it was added to the rationed goods list early on in the war. However, somebody must have complained about the coal miners coming out of the pit thick with coal dust and the miners were made a 'special' case and provided with soap in the baths, stamped with PHB (pithead baths).

By 1941 the houses in Gowland Terrace had been fitted with electricity, which meant that the family didn't need to carry candles around with them during hours of darkness as there was a light in every room. Running water was also an innovation only dreamed of ten years before. Having access to running water made the task of washing day, even without an electric washing machine, much easier. Some of the women, including Bella, still collected rainwater in their poss tubs in the back yard. There was no need to, but it was the way in which they had been brought up, and many continued to use rainwater for their weekly wash as they felt it was a shame to waste it. It still had to be heated up, wherever it came from.

Water, electricity, removal of sewage and household waste were the main areas in which home life had improved by the 1940s due to the growth of local councils. Easington Rural District Council made a determined effort during the difficult 1930s to improve the housing and sanitary conditions in the colliery villages and built 4,700 homes, 2,700 of which replaced the early colliery housing. By the end of the 1930s tied colliery housing had fallen to 25 per cent of the total housing stock in the district. Generally, the people of the mining communities saw this as a good thing. They liked the new council housing with a garden back and front. They liked their indoor flush toilets and bathroom facilities and felt lucky to be able to have them within their village on sites away from the grime, dirt and noise of the pithead. Most of all they liked to have a choice and not be beholden to the coal owners. However, colliery housing was free, it was a perk of the job, and many were prepared to stay in the tied accommodation in order to avoid paying rent.

Billy's mother and his brothers lived in a new council-owned house at No. 120 Wordsworth Avenue. It was very convenient for the working men's club, the new Regal Cinema and the store. After the war, in order to meet the national shortage of housing, the Government introduced temporary prefabricated housing to towns and villages around the country. Wheatley Hill had an estate of prefabs as they became known, at North View, Taylorson Crescent and Patton Crescent. The people moving in couldn't believe the luxury that the prefabs provided compared with the colliery housing they had left; it was even superior to the new council-owned housing. They had large kitchens with a built-in electric ovens and refrigerators – luxuries in the colliery village – a bathroom with a flush toilet, heated towel rail, built-in wardrobes and an airing cupboard. The people who moved into this accommodation loved it and talked about their prefab days fondly for the rest of their lives.

Prefabs (temporary housing), Wheatley Hill.

3

WARTIME WHEATLEY HILL

Despite coal being a vital commodity during the Second World War, and the jobs of coal miners a reserved occupation, many miners from Wheatley Hill were keen to join the armed forces. They were disillusioned by high unemployment rates and general unrest in the coal industry during the 1930s. They were patriotic and willing to volunteer to support their country, in addition to viewing service life as a much more attractive option than working in the troubled coal mines of County Durham.

Those who stayed behind didn't hesitate to become involved in the Home Guard and were encouraged to do so by the colonel of the 22nd Battalion Wheatley Hill Branch and manager of the pit, Mr Joseph Simpson. Billy and his brothers Alf and Herbert walked to Thornley to join the service on the same day in May 1941, after some pressure from their elder brother Luke, who had joined in March. Alf was given an immediate stripe as a result of his (very) short service in the First World War when he was stationed at Tipperary. The other two felt this was very unfair. 'You weren't in the Army five minutes,' Herbert said. 'Aye but thee know a good sowldier when thee see one,' Alf replied.

By the end of 1941 another two of the brothers, Jack and George, had signed up to the Home Guard, with Kit and Norman joining in 1942. All were issued with Home Guard armbands to identify their official role until uniforms became available. Kit was made a sergeant and Norman a lance corporal as a result of their regular Army service, Kit in the Royal Artillery and Norman as a dispatch rider. Brother Aby (Abraham) had joined the Green Howards, often known as the Yorkshire Regiment. He had left Wheatley Hill during the difficult years of the 1920s when mining families suffered many hardships through lack of employment, and obtained employment at the Terry's chocolate factory in York, marrying there in 1931.

A wooden garage next to the colliery offices in Gowland Terrace was available rent-free for the use of the Wheatley Hill branch of the Home Guard. There were further Home Guard headquarters at the bottom of Patton Street in the Temperance Hall and also at Wolmerhausen Street. Most of their duties were looking for windows showing a light, walking the moors looking for fires that may have been lit to attract enemy aircraft and also checking the pit heap for fires, removing ground light sources being of the utmost importance in a time of war.

Rationing was introduced in order that everyone had a fair share of goods that were in short supply, and by July 1940 tea, all fats, jam, cheese and eggs were rationed. Ration books were issued to all members of the family and had to be registered with a shop for basic goods such as sugar, meat, bacon, fat and cheese and wherever the housewife would buy her other foodstuffs from. Bella's was registered with the store.

Gas masks, identity cards and ration books all gave a feeling that the war was real and the blackout became a problem for everyone as blackout curtains became necessary for every window in the home. Street lighting was switched off, vehicle lights were fitted with slotted covers to filter the light downwards, and shop windows were painted black. Cinemas and dance halls were still operating, as generally they had fewer windows than normal domestic buildings and the Regal, the Royalty and the Embassy Ballroom were well attended in Wheatley Hill during the war years.

In August 1940, Wheatley Hill was one of a group of villages on the east coast without military objectives that had military bombs dropped on them by overflying German bombers. The planes probably weren't aiming at anything, but dumping their bombs to gain speed in a bid to get away from RAF fighters. A house in the Dardanelles (the local name for colliery housing streets numbered 1–15) was hit without casualties, and several people were killed while going about their day-to-day business. These included Joseph Pluck from Thornley, killed near the Halfway House public house while he was cycling home from Cassop, and Mr Greenwood, one of the air raid wardens at Wheatley Hill, who was killed carrying out his employment for the Sherburn Hill Co-operative Society at Easington Colliery.

After the attack, the Wheatley Hill Home Guard went up onto the Thornley moor to look for possible fires that may have been sparked by the devices. They found hundreds of incendiary bombs and brought armfuls of unexploded missiles back to the village with them, some keeping them as souvenirs, not realising the danger the items posed.

The Home Guard practised target shooting at a rifle range in Maria Street made by workers at the pit under instructions from the colliery manager. The whole of Maria Street was empty at the beginning of the war and all internal walls had been demolished and targets painted so that the volunteers of the Home Guard and regulars of the West Yorkshire Regiment who were billeted in empty colliery houses could practise their skills.

What wasn't widely known at the time was that an auxiliary unit operational bunker was situated in the woods near to the woodman's cottage on Durham Road. Local medical practitioner Dr MacLean played an active part in the 184th Tunnelling Group billeted there, and a document marked 'secret' was found in his home, Valdigarth in Wheatley Hill front street, after the war. It related to the storage of ammunition underground in the woods. The local men who were part of the group were known as 'The Secret Seven'.

In 1941 an Essential Workers Order was issued that made coal mining a reserved occupation, with miners legally tied to the collieries they worked at for the first time since the abolition of the Miners

Woodmans Cottage, Durham Road.

Bond in 1872. Also, in 1941 the Minister for Labour, Ernest Bevin, called for young women to sign up for work at the shell-filling factories. A propaganda campaign aimed at women told them that they were capable of much more than raising children and running households. Posters and other advertisements encouraged women to help the war effort by signing up for work in the ammunition factories around the country, appealing to their sense of patriotism. Unlike the First World War when the factories were mostly in the towns and poor road links and transport arrangements made travel from the isolated colliery villages impossible, the Second World War provided opportunities for women from the colliery villages to become involved in munitions work. The propaganda surrounding this move centred around carrying out domestic duties at home but incorporating it with some sort of war work. It was very difficult for women to spend their days in factories and then come home to their domestic chores and care-giving roles, but the introduction of initiatives such as British Restaurants, which offered communal feeding or a carry-out service, and the opening of children's nurseries in the colliery villages were all aimed at making it easier for women to work outside of the home and contribute to the war effort by supporting the Home Front.

Margaret Ann Carr (Meggie).

The Carr family were shocked when at the end of 1941, Billy's mother, Meggie – mother to nine sons – signed up to work at the ammunition factory at Aycliffe. She was interviewed by a local newspaper and told the reporter, 'I have been a widow for 22 years and instead of lying about here doing nothing, I might as well be doing my bit. Although I'm 60 I'm very fit and willing and I can fit my housework in when I'm not at the factory.'

Female recruits to Aycliffe were supposed to be under 50, so it is not clear how Meggie, 61 in 1941, managed to gain employment there, but she did and was part of the 16,000 Aycliffe Angels from across County Durham who were transported there by bus and train to work two shifts for the older women and three for the younger ones.

'Well aah hope yer know what yer doin ma. It'll be hard work ye know,' Billy said to his mother when he found out about her war work.

'Aye aah know that and aah'm not frightened of a bit hard work and anyway it's just part time and our Lily works there, and we might even be on the same shift. She'll be a bit company for me.' Lily was Meggie's eldest granddaughter, and Billy wasn't sure she would be over the moon at having her grandmother working alongside her.

An explosives factory at nearby Haswell employed large numbers of women and there was a further factory manufacturing explosives at Aycliffe, about 19 miles away. It was built in 1939 to produce armaments and at its height employed 16,000 people, mostly women. Transport was provided from the colliery villages around the county to take workers to the factory. The facility was very well built with safety in mind and there were over 1,000 buildings scattered over the site. Many of the buildings were protected by mounds of earth to minimise any damage in the event of an explosion and some were built almost entirely underground.

When Billy told Bella about his mother starting at the munitions factory, she said, 'Aye our Hannah says she was interviewed by the papers and there's an article in the Sunday Sun.'

'Eeh aah dinnit believe it, she didn't say a word about being in the papers and aah've just come from there.'

'Why there's nothing to stop her. George and Norman don't take any looking after and aah don't suppose Bill minds. Aah did think she might be too old though. They advertise that women have to be no older than 50.'

'Goodness only knows what she's telt them at Aycliffe,' Billy said.

Bill Langley was Meggie's lodger. Lodgers were an important part of the economy in the colliery villages, especially to a widow, and while she had two sons living at home at the time, Meggie would be expecting them to marry and then she would be dependent on her old age pension as her sole means of income. Having a lodger therefore would improve her financial security and working during wartime couldn't do any harm either.

Gordon was a pupil at Wheatley Hill Boys School during the war and took part in the 'Digging for Victory' initiative in which householders were encouraged to grow vegetables in their gardens to provide

Digging for victory, Wheatley Hill Boys School.

their own food items. The group from his school dug and planted the gardens of the residents in the Aged Miners' Homes.

As well as the war and its problems, the weather at the beginning of 1941 was causing difficulties throughout the Easington District. Wheatley Hill pit was closed for five days, which had never been known. Snow drifts were 8ft deep in places throughout the village, and more importantly the men didn't receive their pay on time as the train lines were closed due to the snow. The people of Wheatley Hill didn't have any post or a bus for over a week and there was no sign of the weather improving. Shops were running low on supplies and soldiers were in the village cutting a road through the snow helped by out-of-work miners.

Billy had hatched a plan that he had obviously given a lot of thought to while he was laid off work and was about to share it with his family. He planned to build an air raid shelter under their sitting room floor. Bella and the boys were surprised and full of questions, all of which Billy could answer, 'Well, aah'm not a pitman for nowt ye naa and aah've learned a thing or two during me time down the pit. Aah thowt aah'd tak part of the passage floor up, to mak a gap of about 4 foot and put a trap door in. Then we'd dig out the space we would need to get down a ladder and under the sitting room with pit props supporting the walls and the ceiling and in case the ceiling in the house collapses while we're down there, we'll get out through an escape route that we'll build to tak us into the garden.'

'Isn't there somebody in Lynn Terrace building an air raid shelter in his garden?' asked Bella

'Aye, it's the cobbler, Tommy Brown, aah was talkin to him in the Beck (the local name for the Colliery Hotel in Lynn Terrace), that's what's give me the idea,' Billy said, 'So, are yer ganna give us a hand?'

Both boys were keen to be involved but realistically most of the work would be done on a weekend as they both had other commitments, Gordon at Wheatley Hill Boys School and Alf serving his electrician apprenticeship at the pit and attending night classes at the A.J. Dawson school, Wingate.

'Aah don't suppose anybody's going to ask me what aah think about this scheme,' Bella said.

'Why aah know you'll be pleased,' Billy replied, 'It means we don't have to go to the shelter at the end of the street if the siren goes off in the middle of the night.'

'Aye well there's that aah suppose but what about all the muck that's going to be trailing through the house in pails? It'll be like Stageybank Fair in that passageway with you three making a mess.'

'We'll tak the carpet runner up in the passage and the pails will be taken out the front door and tipped in the garden, and before you say owt, aah'll use some of it for a rockery, or two. All you have to do is wash the passage floor after every shift.'

'Oh well aah'm pleased you'll be taking the carpet runner up! An aah don't mind washing the floor after you, at least aah know it'll be done properly if aah do it meself.'

'Right, that's settled then, we'll have this job boxed off before ye know it,' said Billy.

Over the next few weeks when they weren't at the pit, school or night classes, but mostly on a weekend, Billy and his two sons worked hard at digging out the earth beneath their passageway and sitting room under No. 3 Gowland Terrace. As planned, pit props were brought from the pit to make the walls and top safe and then the walls were covered with conveyor belting that also came from the pit. The escape route into the garden was constructed and once the small room was finished, Billy built a long deck chair-shaped seat big enough for the four of them. He installed an electric light, and an electric fire was taken down. Friends, family and neighbours all came to see the air-raid shelter and congratulated Billy and his sons on a fine structure.

Billy gave Bella and the boys clear instructions of how to get into the shelter and secure the hatch if the siren sounded when he was out on his Home Guard duties. On the first night it was used, he was out and Bella, her two sons and their dog, Floss, an Airedale terrier, were just going down through the hatch in the passageway when Mrs Smith, their next-door neighbour, knocked on the back door and asked if she could go into the shelter with them. 'Aah reckon aah'll be safer under your floor than under me own kitchen table cos aas not trailing to the end of the street to the shelter,' she said, and for the duration of the war, whenever the air raid siren sounded, Mrs Smith shared the shelter at No. 3 Gowland Terrace.

The 1940s were difficult years both at home and abroad. Billy's brother Aby, who was serving his country as a private in the Green Howards, was killed in action at El-Alamein. His mother, Meggie, was devastated on hearing the news of his death, as were his eight brothers living in Wheatley Hill. Those of them who could visited Aby's wife Holly and their three children in York. They travelled there by train from Thornley Station, but due to a major incident at York Station they had to get off the train at Northallerton and a bus took them into York. Of course, there was no body to bury but Holly had official notice that Aby had been killed on 28 June 1942. There was no question of her coming to Wheatley Hill with her children. She was born and bred in York and would stay there as that's where her family network was and she hardly knew Aby's brothers or his mother, having only met some of them when she married in 1931.

When they got back to Wheatley Hill, the brothers went straight to their mother's house to report on Holly and the children. Meggie was upset and wished she'd gone to York with them. 'Did ye tell Holly to bring the bairns to see me when the war's over?' she said.

'Aye we did ma,' eldest son Luke said, 'and she says she will, it's a shame you haven't seen them yet.'

As he walked home to Gowland Terrace through Wheatley Hill front street, Billy saw the new British Restaurant that had recently opened above the pork butchers shop opposite the Nimmo. Food was very scarce by now and local councils were encouraging people to take part in communal eating in these establishments that were springing up in the colliery villages. The sign outside said you could get a three-course meal and a cup of tea for 11*d* (£4.31 at 2023 prices), so it was perhaps a bit expensive for most pockets. The restaurant would no doubt offer alternatives to the three-course meal but Billy knew that whatever the cost, Bella wouldn't entertain it; she was old-fashioned like that. She would prefer to struggle on with less food and cook it herself. There were spaces for 195 people in the new Wheatley Hill facility and it also offered a carry-out service for those who didn't want to eat in.

British Restaurants were introduced in 1940 initially to provide help where residents had been bombed out of their homes, used up their ration coupons or just needed help; the Labour Party, however, saw them as a permanent solution to guaranteeing a nutritious meal for all and making use of the available food supply. The opening of the British Restaurant at Wheatley Hill in 1942 provided an excellent alternative to home cooking; the main problem for the restaurants was keeping stocked up on cutlery items. Those eating there felt that the cutlery was much better quality than what they had at home, and many took it home with them whenever they stopped off for a meal.

When he got home, Bella wanted to know about the trip to York. She didn't know Holly very well but was sympathetic to her situation. 'Well, it's a good job she's got her folks round her, and she won't be on her own. How old are their bairns now?'

'Why they'll be about 10, 8 and 6. Gordon's the eldest, then Kenny and the little lass is the youngest.'

'Why when the war's over, we'll have to go down to York to see Holly, we'll have to keep in touch with her,' Bella suggested.

'Aye we will, me ma said the same thing and we'll mak sure she brings the bairns here for their holidays to see their Wheatley Hill folks,' Billy said.

Billy went on to tell her about the opening of the British Restaurant in the front street and, as he had predicted, Bella was dead against it, her good mood evaporating quickly. She didn't see why people couldn't use their imagination and their ration books to provide for their families at home. However, what she didn't take into account was that many housewives weren't as prepared as she had been before the war started and had little food stock to fall back on. Also, the attitudes of younger women were changing with regard to working outside of the home and some would be very susceptible to the propaganda put out by the government, through leaflets, posters, radio broadcasts and films. The government message to women was that they were capable of much more than having babies and looking after their families, but Bella was old-fashioned in her thinking and wouldn't dream of going out to work while she had a family to look after. 'There's been too much made of getting married women out of the house and into jobs in this war if you ask me,' she said. 'They've opened a children's nursery up Wordsworth Avenue for women who want to leave their bairns and go and work in factories, and now they've opened a restaurant so that they don't need to cook at home. Where will it all end? What's the matter with staying at home and looking after your family?'

'Why nowt aah suppose, but some women seem to want to be involved in war work. Aah read in the paper that the demands on the women are far greater in this war than they've ever been before.'

'Aye, why they would say that but those demands should be in their own homes dealing with rationing, families and air raids, not in some factory.'

Billy knew when to keep his mouth shut, especially since he had opened the can of worms in the first place, so he thought he would tell her later that the pit had started to sell pies. The canteen building wasn't finished and probably wouldn't be until after the war, but they were doing a roaring trade selling pies from one of the colliery buildings. He thought he should be looking for a suitable gap in the tirade to leave the room and escape to his garden.

Being the youngest daughter of Victorian parents (her mother was 45 and her father 47 when Bella was born) brought attitudes and values that Bella took with her on her journey through life and it was not unusual therefore that she would think a married woman working outside the home wasn't the done thing. It was from her old-fashioned values that she maintained her self-respect and gained pride in her achievements of creating a happy and well-ordered home with well-tested routines and was proud of the quality of her household management. These things were important to Bella as they had been to previous generations, and although times were changing with regard to the role of women in society, they stayed the same for her.

As an efficient house keeper who had listened to the reports of the likelihood of a world war and taken government advice to do so, Bella had built up a good stock of store cupboard staples, such as flour, sugar, tea and other dried goods. She had always conserved Billy's garden produce; she made jam with the rhubarb and strawberries, dried and stored peas, hung onions in a dry and dark place, stored potatoes similarly and pickled beetroot and smaller onions, so when rationing hit some families hard, Bella had her stock of goods safe and sound, ensuring her family wouldn't starve in the short term. She had always picked blackberries during the autumn to make jam and continued to do this at Wheatley Hill. Billy had dug up all of his flower beds, which was a disappointment to both of them, and planted vegetables for the table, which became a necessity.

Billy continued to keep two pigs at Wheatley Hill in the allotments behind Gowland Terrace with Billy Raffell from Smith Street. They had two pigs each and took turns in raising two and killing two. They did the killing and the curing themselves. The curing was done by rubbing salt all over it and leaving it for six weeks. The meat was shared between the two families and then hung on hooks in the scullery, and as rationing became really strict, the pig meat and its by-products of pease pudding, black pudding, brawn etc. were a godsend.

Slaughtering had become an issue at the beginning of the war, and the forty or so slaughterhouses operating throughout the Easington District were closed, so the slaughtering of livestock was carried out at Station Town Co-operative Store so that it could be regulated by the Ministry of Food. However, for those rearing and killing a pig for their own consumption, and if they held a licence, the practice could continue. The applications for licences throughout the Easington District for keeping pigs rose steadily during the war from sixty-nine in 1940 to 782 in 1946. Therefore, pork was the joint for Christmas day throughout the war years for the Carr family.

Rationing was a nightmare for Meggie, who wasn't able to stock-pile food items, so Billy and Bella helped out where they could with produce from the garden and the pig. Billy used to joke, 'Aah bet aah's not the only one of the lads helping me ma out, but she never lets on. She'll probably be better fed than any of us.'

Housewives found it very difficult to feed their families using the meagre rations, but they were able to pool their individual allowances in order to give better portions to those who needed them. The meat-based diet favoured by mining families before the war had to be adjusted to whatever was available, with a big emphasis on vegetables and potatoes in particular.

Christmas During Wartime

Preparing for Christmas during wartime became more difficult as the war progressed. After the announcement of war on 3 September 1939 there was very little missing from Christmas celebrations that year. Fruit and vegetables were plentiful and while everyone knew that rationing was due to start in January 1940, no one seemed to take any notice and all seemed determined to have a good Christmas. The only things that reminded them that they were at the beginning of a war was the blackout and the number of men missing from the village.

Wartime Christmases after 1939 were more difficult as food being imported by sea was often sunk by German naval vessels and for the remainder of the war Christmas was a make-do-and-mend affair, no different from the rest of the war years.

Throughout the training period of her girlhood and without knowing any different, Bella lived by the make-do-and-mend methods instilled into her and her sisters by their mother. They were taught to be economical in everything they did, not as a result of war but as a result of necessity and the poor wages brought home by their father in low-paid work at the pit due to him having an eye complaint. Susan and her daughters were practical and skilful over a range of areas and so during the shortages of the 1920s, '30s and of wartime rationing in the '40s, Bella conducted her style of housekeeping as she always had done, looking for the best ways in which to use her raw materials wisely, not throwing anything away that could be reused, whether it be food or clothing, and making sure no one in her family went without. She saved the paper bags that her food came in and opened her Christmas presents very carefully in order not to damage the paper so that she could use it for her Christmas wrappings next year. Christmas cards were kept and the pictures on the front cut out to make gift tags for future Christmas gifts. And so when this was a massive requirement of everyone, particularly those responsible for running a household during the Second World War, it required very little extra effort from Bella.

She continued to 'turn' her sheets when they became threadbare in the middle. This involved cutting them down the middle, turning the outside edges into the middle and joining them together with a centre seam. She never threw clothing away; she could remodel her own clothes by taking them in, letting them out, adding a panel or a vent, always removing and saving buttons and unpicking seams etc. to allow the material to be reused, and at the end of 1941 when clothing was rationed, she was very pleased that she had a stock of wool and material. For several months before Christmas, Bella was busy planning how to turn her supplies into 'new' clothing as suitable presents for her family. For someone who had lived through the First World War as Bella had, this wasn't a great deal of hardship as she could remember making Christmas presents for her family then too. Wrapping paper wasn't available, so presents for immediate family weren't wrapped at all and presents going out of the family were given in brown paper or *The Daily Herald*.

With her stored sugar supply, Bella was also able to continue to make ginger beer for the festivities. It required mostly sugar (1lb) and water with a bit of ground ginger and cream of tartare as well as a small amount of dried yeast. It could be ready within two days and provided a treat for the family over the festive season.

She did her best to make the house look festive. Son Alf had bought a Christmas tree a few years earlier and it came out to be decorated. Usually, the Christmas cards would add to the festive feel of the home, but by 1941 they were small and printed on flimsy paper. Bella had managed to get some coloured gummed paper and made paper chains, enough to decorate their sitting room, giving it a Christmassy look. Also as a result of her thrifty ways, ever since foil tops came into use for milk bottles, she had saved every single one, which she washed carefully and dried and stored in a biscuit tin until in 1941, feeling that she had enough, she threaded them onto thick cotton and hung them around the walls of the sitting room as Christmas decorations. Most were silver but there were a few gold tops in among the decorations, and they made a swishing noise when a door opened, as they were caught in the draught. Together with several old cardboard Santa Claus decorations, the house in Gowland Terrace was very festive. A fire was lit in the sitting room and on Christmas morning the smell of roasting pork and the sage and onion stuffing created a Christmasy feel. The home-made decorations looked attractive, the foil milk bottle tops glistening as the firelight caught them. Even their unwrapped presents looked charming tied with coloured ribbon that Bella had collected over the years, and she would continue to use in future years as she rescued it after the gifts were opened. She and Billy didn't buy presents for one another, but the boys had combined their money to get their parents a present. It was an ornament for the sideboard for Bella and a new pipe for Billy. Alf had saved money from his pocket money and Gordon from his milk round with Tommy Buxton.

Ekco A77 all electric radio.

Billy and Bella had bought an Ekco A77 all electric radio in 1936 so that they could listen to the Coronation, and during the war began to listen to the news bulletins broadcast at the end of the day. Since 1939 King George VI had broadcast his Christmas message, and during wartime people were anxious to hear what he had to say. It became the highlight of Christmas Day. Christmas was famous for reflection and this year it was brought home to everyone in the Carr household just how lucky they were, still being able to listen to the King on their wireless set with the amount of fighting going on around the world involving family, friends, neighbours and workmates.

4

EXPECTATIONS

Bella saw parenting as part of her domestic duties and she was keen for her sons to achieve. Men usually left the parenting decisions to their wives, but both her and Billy shared this ambition for their sons. They had each received an education appropriate to their working-class roots during the early 1900s, Billy at the board school in Wheatley Hill front street and Bella at Ludworth school. One of the major themes of their education was patriotism and the importance of the Empire introduced into the curriculum after the Balfour 1902 Education Act that also introduced local education authorities. Their education was concentrated on daily lessons in arithmetic, reading and writing that were developed through topics such as history, geography and religious studies and weekly topics of nature study, singing, woodwork for boys and knitting and sewing for girls. They were taught in large classes with evidence of tough discipline recorded in punishment books. They would witness the use of dunces' caps, lines, detention and most commonly the cane. This was an education aimed at preparing children from mining and other working-class families for lives as subordinate workers.

Mr and Mrs Jopling were proud of the achievements of Bella and her sisters at Ludworth school. Jake and Susan were the first generation of their families to receive a formal education that taught them both to read and write. They could see the benefit of education for their daughters, even though there were many mining families that did not, feeling education for a girl was a waste of time as she was unlikely to become a breadwinner.

Being the third eldest of nine brothers, there wasn't such an emphasis on education in Billy's family, and he wanted to follow his two older brothers into the workplace as early as possible, which was when he was aged 13 if he passed the Labour Certificate examination. He would not be encouraged to stay at school by his parents, who had nine sons at home: the more sons in work, the less of a financial burden it was looking after them. Billy knew he wouldn't be able to work at the pit, which was his ultimate ambition, until he was 15, but felt he could better use his time in employment rather than school, so he applied to sit the Labour Certificate examination that was held at the Robert Richardson Grammar School, Ryhope. Success at this examination would mean that he could leave his education and enter the world of work. On the day of the examination in May 1916, Billy walked from Wheatley Hill to Ryhope, sat the examination and walked home again (a round trip of about 24 miles). He and Wheatley Hill School were notified in July that he had been successful and he was overjoyed that he could leave school to start his working life at Greenhills Farm near Thornley Crossings. He would be 13½ years old and his pay was 2s 6d (12½p) per day, which was considered a good wage for a boy of his age. He was involved in general farming tasks – milking, ploughing, harvesting, mucking out and delivering the milk. He started work at 5.30 a.m. and in the summer months didn't get home until 8 p.m. His working week was six and a half days, his only time off on a Sunday afternoon.

Greenhills Farm.

Most parents in the colliery villages at this time didn't have any ambition for their children beyond seeing their sons in regular employment, preferably in a job that didn't involve going down the pit. In this respect the store and building trades offered alternatives, but inevitably the pit was where most ended up. Girls were encouraged into some sort of domestic service, either at home or at 'place', or perhaps nursing where the skills of running a household learned from their mother were put to good use in return for payment. Boys were of benefit to a family as a result of the wages they could bring into the household and girls for the help with domestic chores they could provide for their mother. Bella had worked in domestic service at a private school in Redcar during the First World War and then for the school master Mr White at Ludworth, keeping house, until she married. These were typical aspirations and expectations of young people of their class and generation.

During the 1920s a debate was taking place across England concerning the introduction of a secondary education for all children, irrespective of their class, but there were many objections to the move.

The Hadow Reports into Education in 1923 showed a progressive attitude to the education of girls, probably for the first time, and the report was also responsible for suggesting that education should be divided into two distinct phases to be called primary and secondary, with the break between the two being at age 11. This was implemented in 1925 and the education system became known as 'junior' and 'senior' education, but entry to the 'secondary' school was by selection as it was considered a waste of money to try and further the education of those who were not capable.

The opening of a secondary school to serve east Durham in 1930 was a major step forward for the children of mining families. The school was opened by County Councillor Peter Lee at Wellfield Road, Wingate, and it was named A.J. Dawson School after a previous Director of Education for Durham, with 360 places for children from the villages of Castle Eden, Hutton Henry, Station Town, Wingate, Trimdon, Wheatley Hill, Shotton, Thornley, Ludworth, Haswell and Easington Village. Such a school gave both boys and girls access to careers other than coal mining or domestic work if they did well at school and it was the first time that opportunities were available to the children of mining families from the Easington District that could put them on a par with other communities not dependent on coal. The A.J. Dawson school became a grammar school in 1932 and provided a great advantage to the relatively small numbers that were given the opportunity of this type of education towards facilitating their social mobility. It could be the gateway to a new life. A life away from the pits.

In 1936 Billy and Bella were very proud when their eldest son Alf passed the two-part School Certificate entrance examination that meant he was awarded a place at the A.J. Dawson School. Billy bought a set of ten volumes of *The Children's Encyclopedia* edited by Arthur Mee from a door-to-door salesman to coincide with Alf's success and he saw the purchase as a good investment in the education of his sons, the cost being spread over several months. The books focused on a Christian way of life, a love of Great Britain and the great benefits of the British Empire.

Employment opportunities for boys were almost all related to the pit, but Billy Carr had made it clear to both of his sons from an early age that he wouldn't allow either of them to leave school and work at the pit unless they followed a trade within the coal industry, which is what they both chose to do, Alf as an electrician and Gordon as a mechanical fitter. Gordon often remarked that although his father's education had ended prematurely and by choice at age 13, he was always able to help the boys with their homework from school and later on from the night classes they were both following in line with their chosen trades at the pit.

When it was Gordon's time to sit the two-part School Certificate entrance examination, he did well in the first part but didn't pass the second and admitted later that he probably didn't put as much effort into it as he should because he could see the amount of homework that his brother had from the A.J. Dawson School. Therefore Gordon attended Wheatley Hill Boys School, leaving in 1942 to start his apprenticeship as a fitter at Wheatley Hill pit. He wasn't sorry to be leaving school and was looking forward to life as a working man.

Gordon wasn't like Alf. He did what he had to do to get what he wanted, but he wasn't ambitious. He found the studying required for his engineering certificates tedious and was disappointed that the course content wasn't linked closely to coal mining engineering but was of a general engineering nature. He felt that if the content of the night classes courses had been more closely related to his job at the pit it would have been a massive incentive to enjoy and commit to the learning with more enthusiasm. Nevertheless, he completed his seven-year apprenticeship successfully, starting as a fully qualified fitter at Wheatley Hill pit in 1949.

Both Alf and Gordon were encouraged into taking part in planned activities outside of the home and as children both attended piano accordion lessons at Sherburn Village once a week. They both had some involvement in the local cricket team, spending time at the Wheatley Hill cricket ground after school when they were growing up and both representing the second team on occasions. After the war, and along with their father, they both had season tickets for

Sunderland football club. They visited the cinemas in Wheatley Hill at least twice a week and were also involved in the social activities provided by the Wesleyan Chapel where their friends went.

With three workers in the house, Bella was able to budget and save effectively. Both boys were on the same system as their father in that their wages were handed over to their mother and she gave them pocket money. Neither seemed to mind. She bought their clothes, they never went short of anything, and they enjoyed a family holiday every year. Their pocket money was spent on trips to the pictures, sometimes twice a week, and visits to the live theatre at Hartlepool or Sunderland where they sometimes saw their next-door neighbour from Cooper's Terrace, Thornley, Ernie Stoddart, who was a performer.

Gordon Carr and his piano accordion.

As with her own parents, Bella and Billy shared a good partnership with clear divisions. Billy, like Bella's own father, could be described as a 'good' man. He was responsible for providing the money from his pay packet, which he did willingly every week, handing the whole to Bella and being happy to receive pocket money. He was a moderate, social drinker and a weekend gambler who liked to bet on the horses but, more importantly, he was a family man who valued his wife and recognised her efforts in the home and he provided an excellent role model for his sons. He was also responsible for their garden, although this was something of a shared interest between them. It was Billy who did the bulk of the work, particularly with the vegetables, Bella preferring to look after the flowerbeds. She was responsible for the smooth running of the home and for making Billy's life at home as trouble-free as possible so that he could concentrate on his job at the pit. She was the financial controller, responsible for saving and spending. In this respect she could choose sensible spending options via weekly payment methods from the many travellers who visited the colliery villages and by using her dividend at the store, which could be used for a variety of high-value purchases.

5

ROUTINES

In common with the rest of the colliery village, Monday continued to be washing day into the 1940s and even though it was now a much easier task with water on tap than it had been in her mother's day, Bella continued to collect water in her poss tub to heat up in the set pot attached to the fire. This meant that cooking was kept to a minimum on washing day and the Monday meal was usually Sunday's leftovers, known as caad-waarmed-up. This was always accompanied by mint salad – finely chopped leafy green lettuce leaves, mint leaves, chopped scallions and a spoonful of sugar all mixed with vinegar. While this was also served with the Sunday dinner, the Carr family thought it was much better with their Monday dinner. Bella didn't have an electric washing machine until the early 1960s and so the clothes were possed in the same way as they had been for generations. Having her own back yard, however, meant that she could hang the washing out to dry and there was no danger of any delivery vehicles disturbing the clothes prop that raised the clothes up to allow them to billow and dry. The only disadvantage of living so near to the pithead was the fine black mist that descended when the pulley wheels were working and attached itself to the drying washing. A wet washing day was a miserable experience for everyone in the household. Bella had a very tall clothes horse and if she couldn't hang the washing in the back yard, it was hung on this, which was positioned around the coal fire in the kitchen. As it was a priority to dry the clothes, no one in the family felt any warmth from the coal fire that they could have done with on a wet day. No one liked a wet washing day.

Billy always worked in the first shift (or forst shift as the Durham miners pronounced it). This descended (to the pit bottom) at 3 a.m. and ascended (to the surface) at 11 a.m. Billy was happy to see himself out to work. Bella would make his bait the night before, usually a jam sandwich, and he would have a cup of tea and a slice of bread before leaving the house at about 2.50 a.m. When he came out of the pit he would wash at the pit baths, leaving his pit clothes in a locker there and come home clean to have a meal, which was usually a dinner, and go to bed until about 4 p.m. The running of the household was greatly inconvenienced by a sleeping miner in the cottage-type housing, but in the two-up two-down houses of Gowland Terrace, normal family life could continue, within reason, as the family were well away from the bedroom and less likely to disturb his sleep.

Bella did her ironing on a Tuesday, and even at the beginning of the 1940s preferred to use the flat irons that she had been taught to iron with. These were heated up near the fire and then their heat transferred to the clothes. Women using the flat irons had to have their wits about them, as the handles became really hot and many a hand was burned by forgetting to use a cloth (or kettle holder) around the handle to pick the iron up with. While carrying out the ironing, Bella also assessed whether or not any of the clothes needed mending and if they did these were set aside to be tackled later. She had a very small portable sewing machine by this time, bought from the traveller, Mr Graham, who represented the same Sunderland department store that had visited her mother at Ludworth. He came every Friday to collect any money Bella owed him and it was an opportunity for her to order further items, which she usually did at Christmas. Purchases through the traveller meant that housewives could spread the cost of large items without having to save up for them.

Wednesday was a baking day, all cooking being carried out on the fire or in the coal oven attached to the fire. It was normally the day that meat was delivered by the store butcher from the Sherburn Hill Co-operative Stores in Wheatley Hill. He came around with his horse cart twice a week, Wednesday and Saturday morning, and the women bought their meat for the weekend as well as any other meat products they might need. In Bella's case, she used the pork products from their pigs but ordered pie meat, a cheaper cut of beef, for her meat and tattie pies. She always made these in two sizes, tea plate size and saucer size. She stewed the beef and onion until it was succulent and then mixed it with mashed potatoes and assembled her pies. Jam tarts and ned cakes were also part of the Wednesday baking day, which focused on pastry items. However, during wartime and with so little butcher meat to be had, baking day was a very boring affair as far as savoury goods were concerned. Spam was available and she had the bacon and meat from their pig but Bella continued to make her meat and tattie pies; she just left the meat out and replaced it with turnip!

On a Thursday morning, it was her big day out to visit the Sherburn Hill Co-operative store, where she might need household or clothing items. All clothes for Billy and the boys were purchased by Bella at the store. She chose them, brought them home and they wore them without question. She put her coat on top of her wrap-around pinnie and of course always wore her hat. She wouldn't be seen out of the house without a hat. As a shareholder at the store, Bella got most of her family's need there. For everything she spent she gave her store number; her purchases were recorded in a book in the department of the sale and she was given a receipt for each item purchased. At the end of the day all purchases made that day would be recorded into the store ledgers and at the end of each quarter of the year the dividend was calculated on the amount of purchases made by each customer. The Sherburn Hill Co-operative Society was well known for offering the highest rate of dividend and it provided a good savings scheme for many households, perhaps the only savings scheme some could manage. If she could do without it, Bella left her divi in for as long as she could and if the family needed any larger-value items, the divi could be put to good use.

Wheatley Hill front street.

She would leave Gowland Terrace at about 11.30 a.m. on a Thursday morning after Billy came in from the pit, had his meal and got off to bed. She walked along the end of the colliery rows past Elizabeth Street, John Street, Smith Street etc., turning up Patton Street and then along Ford Street, Church Street and into the main shopping street in the village, which was still known as 'The Farm' by older residents as it contained Rock Farm, the oldest building in the village. The Store was at the far end of the front street on Thornley Road and Bella enjoyed looking through the various departments – furniture, clothes, shoes, hardware. Before and after the war the store man visited Co-operative customers at the beginning of the week with his long order book that listed all food items that could be delivered. The customer would tell him what she wanted, and it would be ticked off his list to be delivered by the end of the week. However, during wartime this system was temporarily suspended as the range of foodstuffs available was very limited. It was a greatly missed service as it meant that housewives were out shopping more regularly for rationed goods and other products as they were limited as to what they could carry during one visit.

All shops including the store had long, slow-moving queues for every food type. There was a queue at the dairy section, a queue at the dried goods section, a queue at the butcher's counter etc. Shopping during wartime took such a long time and by the time ration books had been checked, orders placed and goods wrapped in their greaseproof paper etc., it could take well over an hour to obtain one or two items.

If she had plenty of time, Bella would pop in to see Mrs Carr, Billy's mother, who lived at No. 120 Wordsworth Avenue. One or more of her sisters-in-law were often visiting at this time, and it was a good time for them to get together to hear the gossip, family or otherwise. As well as the usual talk about the lack of food due to rationing and particularly the scarcity of fresh fruit, the talk at the beginning of 1941 was the exciting news that Barbara, the wife of Billy's elder brother, Alf, had given birth to twin boys. 'Well as far as aah know there's no twins in our family, so it must be in Baab's. Anyway, they've called one after our Norman and the other Richard after her da. She'll have her work cut out with two babies but the older lasses, our Lily and Doreen will be a good help with the other bairns.'

During these get-togethers there was always speculation about when Billy's youngest brothers George and Norman would marry. 'Why thee don't tell me anything and they've never brought any lasses back here, so your guess is as good as mine but now our Norman's joined the Army, aah'm not expecting him to be getting married any time soon.'

Bella enjoyed these meetings at the home of her mother-in-law. Her own mother had died in 1940 and she missed the daily contact with her. Mrs Carr's house was not well-ordered like her own, and she didn't follow the strict routines that Bella did, but it was comfortable and welcoming. The kettle was always on, and numerous cups of tea were drunk throughout the day due to the location of the house opposite the store, with friends and family calling in regularly while they were doing their shopping. It did bring into question Meggie's tea ration and how she was able to provide for her high number of visitors though.

When she returned home on a Thursday, Bella got straight on with her housework. She always cleaned the sitting room on a Thursday and, once Billy was out of bed, the bedrooms.

Friday, as was a tradition among the mining families, was spent preparing for the weekend. The kitchen, the main room in the house, was cleaned from top to bottom, furniture polished, mats taken out and beaten, brasses and fenders polished, the fireplace black-leaded and steps both back and front washed. In the afternoon Bella could be seen sweeping the back yard and the area outside the back gate the width of the house before swilling both with soapy water. These were the same routines she had followed since she was a little girl helping her mother in their home at Ludworth and were probably the same as those followed by her grandmother. Some things had changed, but the routines remained the same for many coal mining families and particularly for Bella as she carried out her allocated tasks, always singing softly to herself.

It was from listening to her as she worked that I became familiar with snatches of 1930s songs as she sang the lyrics 'Little man you're crying, I know why you're blue, someone stole your kiddy-car away'. This was part of a much longer song but that is the only line I know from my grandma's repertoire. She also sang, 'He flies through the air with the greatest of ease, the daring young man on the flying trapeze' and another, 'Darling I am growing old, silver threads amongst the gold'. I only ever heard her sing these lines; she probably didn't know the rest of the songs, but she sang them throughout my childhood and her repertoire was never added to by more modern songs. I remember discussing the singing with my cousin Hilary when we were about 8 or 9 years old and we came to the conclusion that our grandma must be happy as people don't normally sing when they're not happy.

She loved Saturday afternoons. Billy and the boys went out after dinner on a Saturday. Before the war it would be to watch local football and after the war they had season tickets for Sunderland. When the team were playing at Roker Park they would be there supporting, and on the weeks when Sunderland were away from home, Billy and the lads supported any of the other local teams that were at home – Middlesbrough, Newcastle or Hartlepool. Saturday afternoon was Bella's time as it had been when she lived at home with her mother and sisters. Their da had always made himself scarce on a Saturday, probably to Polly Vasey's his local pub (the Standish Arms) at Ludworth. Their mother would put the tin bath in front of the fire and place the clothes horse hung with blankets around it for privacy and she and the girls would take turns having their weekly bath. So, whenever Bella had a Saturday afternoon to herself, she brought the big tin bath into the kitchen, set it in front of the fire and filled it with hot water, locked the door, closed the curtains and had a bath, listening to the wireless while she soaked.

After tea on a Saturday and Sunday night, Bella took her pinny off. They were the only two nights in the week when she could be seen, after tea on both nights, relaxing with her family without her pinny. Weekends were still valued in the mining communities because it was the only time the families could spend quality time together, and this was particularly the case as Sunday dinner continued to be highly regarded. While Bella was busy preparing the Sunday dinner, Billy went to the Beck, the local name for the Colliery Hotel in Lynn Terrace, or the Nimmo Hotel in the front street for a pint. However, in wartime of course this depended on whether either of the public houses had any beer to sell. Billy would be sure to meet one or more of his brothers in the pub on a Sunday but was always home for his dinner, which would be put on the table at 1.30 p.m. Sunday dinner during wartime consisted mainly of vegetables from the garden, including steepy peas, an onion pudding that didn't require any eggs instead of Yorkshire pudding, and probably pork and crackling from their own pig, sage and onion stuffing, accompanied of course by mint salad with ingredients from their garden.

After they had had their tea on a Sunday, Bella, Billy and the two boys often went to Ludworth to visit Bella's sister and her family, and they never went empty-handed. Billy always had something to share with them from his garden or the pig. Hannah kept hens at Ludworth and she often had eggs for Bella to take home, and these gifts were appreciated, especially during wartime. If they had plenty of fuel they went on the motorbike and sidecar or walked along the Thornley moor on summer nights.

Hannah and Jack lived in one of the new council-built houses in Barnard Avenue. It gave the boys time to catch up with their cousins, although their elder cousin Leslie was now married and had a son of his own, young Jack, and cousin Rene had recently married and was now training as a nurse at Ryhope hospital, but was usually visiting her parents on a Sunday evening. There was always a good atmosphere as the two families crammed into the small modern house. It was easier for the Wheatley Hill family to travel to Ludworth than the much bigger Ludworth family travelling to Wheatley Hill. Billy and Jack went to the Queens Head for a pint while the rest of the family caught up with each other's news. Hannah's daughters Rene and Mavis made the supper in time for the men coming back from the pub. At one memorable supper, Hannah said to her husband Jack, 'By you're eating a lot of bread the night.'

He replied, 'Aye why aah's trying te mop this egg up off the plate with it.'

'Why you better get another loaf then,' Hannah said, ''cos that's a picture of a yellow flower on the plate, not an egg.' Everyone laughed at Jack's failing eyesight, probably made worse by a few pints of beer.

Bella still thought of Ludworth as home and valued her weekly visits to her sister and her family.

Devastating news hit the family in 1944 when Sid Young, the husband of Bella's niece, Nora, died. He was only 37 and left Nora with three little girls, the youngest just 3. 'Aah'll have to go over to see if aah can help our Nora out a bit,' Bella said. 'When you get up tomorrow afternoon, we'll have a ride over Murton if you've got plenty coupons for petrol.'

Bella's sister Hannah wasn't in the best of health and was unable to make the journey to Murton. Hannah had suffered severe health problems after the birth of her son Norman in 1914, and while she went on to have another two children, the illness returned periodically as she got older, and she was often bedridden for short periods. Nora's sister Stella had her hands full with her little boy, Harold, who also had health problems, so she wasn't in a position to help her sister out either, and her brother Douglas was serving with the Royal Army Medical Corps (RAMC) in Wales.

Nora and Sidney Young, 1931.

Having lost her own mother when she was just 11, Nora was brought up by Bella's mother. There was only a six year age gap between Nora and Bella and Nora thought of Bella and Hannah as her older sisters. She was particularly pleased to see her aunt after having suffered the loss of her husband. Always practical, Bella took with her some of her own tea ration for the visitors Nora would get over the next few days, vegetables from the garden and a joint of pork loin that Nora could cut up into bacon rashers over the coming days.

As was usual at the time of a family death, the curtains were closed at Nora's house and the three little girls were quiet when Bella and Billy arrived, the smallest one, Beatrice, not understanding what was going on. The eldest, Nora, was 12 and the middle one, Marion, 8, and they knew what had happened to their da. Nora and Sid had lived at Murton since their marriage in 1931 and she had a good support network as Sid was from a close-knit Murton family who were more than happy to help her out at this very sad time. Sid's death was unexpected. He had TB, and while the family knew it would restrict him from working underground at the pit, no one expected him to die as quickly as he did. Nora told Bella he had died of meningitis.

'The same as our Stella's little lad?' Bella asked. 'Aye the doctor says it's an infection and because Sid was bad with TB, he couldn't fight it even though he was in the Royal Infirmary at Sunderland.'

'Aah've heard me ma say that me grandma lost three or four bairns to TB, but that was years ago, you'd think they'd have come up with a cure by now, wouldn't you?'

'Aye why thee haven't and we didn't have the right food for him either with all this rationing.'

Sid actually died of tuberculous meningitis, an illness that strikes when a patient with tuberculosis develops a further infection that attacks either the central nervous system or the brain. Early detection of the secondary infection is crucial to the survival of the patient, and Sid died in hospital where the medical profession were trying to treat his condition.

'Eeh aah don't know how aah'm ganna manage,' Nora said, over and over again between her tears.

'Yer strong our Nora and you'll have to manage, ye've got them little lasses to think about. Ye've got plenty folks round you who want to help and don't be frightened to ask. Sid's family have always been good to you. Did ye have him insured?'

'Aye with the Prudential, there'll be plenty to pay for the funeral.'

'Why that's a blessing,' Bella said, 'it's one thing less for ye to worry about.'

Bella and Billy stayed for a couple of hours and Nora was upset to see her aunt go but knew she would return for the funeral. Even though she was close to Sid's family, there was nothing like your own family at times like this.

The lads had the table set when they got home, and Bella set about making their tea. She fried bacon and boiled some cabbage and potatoes she'd left steeping in water, and they were soon sitting down to eat. Alf was in a hurry to eat his tea as he was due at his night classes. Gordon was two years into his fitter's apprenticeship at Wheatley Hill pit but never had much to say about it. He too attended night classes at Hartlepool College but tonight wasn't one of them. 'How's our Nora and the little lasses?' Alf asked.

'Oh, she's upset, naturally, but she knows she'll have to get on with it for the sake of the bairns. Sid's family are good and aah think she'll have plenty company through the day, but when there's only her and the bairns are in bed, that's when it'll hit her hard.'

'Aah think he must have been bad for a few months,' Billy said. 'He was on surface work at the pit, and that's unusual for a lad of his age.'

'Aye he had a bad chest, but the doctor thought it would clear up if he stayed out of the coal dust, but it didn't, and it wasn't just a bad chest, it was TB. Will our Nora get any compensation?'

'Only if they can prove his bad chest and death was due to the coal dust,' Billy said, 'Aah don't think it's likely but if you believe what you read in the papers, that might all change after the war.'

6

AFTER THE WAR

Normal didn't become reality until August 1945 when the war was eventually declared to be over. The pit buzzer blew to announce the good news as families took down the blackout curtains and breathed a sigh of relief. There was an air of party throughout the village. The ladies of Wheatley Terrace and Cain Terrace organised a party for sixty-six children, who were fed and given a sixpence (2½p) each. Mrs Mather made and iced the Victory cake. There was an outdoor event at the New Tavern, Wingate Lane, where the villagers sang and danced outside the pub until the early hours of the morning. However, there was also an air of concern among the older miners, those who could remember the crippling depression after the First World War, and despite government reassurances that things were about to change massively for the working classes, that concern remained. However a Labour government, elected in 1945 and led by Clement Attlee, caused great excitement throughout the mining communities, so perhaps things were about to change?

Gordon couldn't wait for the end of the war. He felt he had just about talked his father into buying a car once fuel rationing stopped. Brother Alf was just as keen but hadn't been on the same mission as

Gordon to bring it up at every opportunity. Since starting his apprenticeship at the pit, Gordon had been working alongside Lenny Dinsley, a mechanical fitter and father of Gordon's friend Ronnie. Lenny was interested in cars and offered to look out for a good second-hand one for the family. Billy gave him the go-ahead, Bella agreeing as long as they would teach her to drive. Gordon didn't think this was very likely but agreed it was an excellent idea, recognising that any opposition could halt the purchase!

Eventually, towards the end of 1945, Lenny found a good second-hand Ford 8 at Darlington. Billy, Gordon and Lenny travelled to Darlington by bus to see the car and after taking Lenny's advice, Billy bought it. He didn't know anything about cars and wasn't particularly interested, but he could see the benefit of being able to travel independently, as the family had with their motorbike and sidecar, which he could now sell to offset the cost of the car. Due to Bella's good financial management, Billy was able to pay cash for the car and Lenny drove them home to Wheatley Hill, where it was parked outside the house at Gowland Terrace and became their pride and joy.

Bella with the Ford 8, 1945.

Billy and his sons learned to drive, although Billy didn't enjoy it and was happy for his sons to share that task, and the two boys took on the responsibility for the mechanics of keeping the car on the road. Teaching their mother to drive wasn't high on the agenda of the two boys, although Billy did take her out for a few driving lessons. However, as she didn't become one of the regular drivers of the car, we may assume that she lost interest?

In 1946 my dad applied for a Private Hire Operator's Licence and used my granda's car to take local people on holiday. He did this for quite a few years and built up a list of regular customers travelling to destinations such as Blackpool, the Lake District and Gilsland, close to Hadrian's Wall, usually in the pit holidays but also for long weekends such as Easter.

Billy applied for planning permission to build a garage to park the car in at the end of Gowland Terrace and when the permission was granted he found that wood was still in short supply and didn't know what he would build it with. Eventually he managed to get hold of some wooden crates used to transport glass and used them to build a very substantial garage with an inspection pit.

The Labour Party produced its manifesto in preparation for a general election towards the end of the war and called it 'Let Us Face the Future'. It contained action to ensure full employment, the nationalisation of key industries, an urgent housing programme, a national health service and social provision that had been suggested by Liberal William Beveridge. A new education system was set up by the wartime coalition government in 1944 and had already been introduced. The government felt that the British people deserved a new start, and the changes were intended to improve the lives of everyone.

Nationalisation of key industries was aimed at creating a fairer system of providing jobs so that men would be in full employment and able to provide for their families. The coal industry was one of the industries included in the scheme and on 1 January 1947, Nationalisation (Vesting) Day was celebrated in the mining villages. Despite another harsh winter, fuel shortages, a wage freeze and financial crisis, the miners of the Easington District and Seaham Parliamentary Division were

New gate sign at Wheatley Hill pit, 1 January 1947.

celebrating the end of the private coal owners and looking forward to a brighter future. Some signs mounted outside coal mines throughout the country announced government ownership of the pits and read 'managed by the National Coal Board on behalf of the people'.

Almost all the points made in the Labour Party manifesto became reality by the end of the decade; only housing didn't meet its objective. Housing became a massive problem across the country after the war due to bombing in the industrial towns of the midlands and the south and a large stock of poor-quality housing that was becoming unacceptable in all areas of the country, including the mining villages of County Durham, as the government were trying to improve living conditions for all. Council house building had begun before the war and already-started estates were completed after it, but the council's main contribution to post-war housing was in the supply of temporary prefabricated buildings available for rent. The New Towns Act, passed by the government in 1946, was in response to the housing shortage, but poor-quality housing and living conditions continued into the 1950s and '60s throughout the country.

It became part of the government's vision to build new towns across the country, creating self-contained communities with well-designed housing on open field sites offering local employment to a large percentage of their population. This was felt to be preferable to building new housing in individual villages. The vision for the building of a new town in the east Durham area (from a government point of view) was to move communities away from the coal pits with their waste heaps, dilapidated buildings, dilapidated land and its poor-quality housing where the smell, smoke and noise of the pits was always present and difficult to get away from. Psychologically, the planners felt, it was a bad thing to be on top of your work, and much worse if it was in the conditions of a mining village. They were anxious to point out that women and children also lived in these conditions, which need not continue when there was the alternative of a new town that would provide new housing along with the other essential amenities necessary to maintain a good life. One of the main objectives for the new town would be to provide industrial employment in factories for women as it was intended to designate the whole area as a development area in order to encourage light industry.

Mr C.W. Clarke, son of a colliery manager and Chief Engineer and Surveyor for Easington District Council, was against council investment for individual villages and had been since at least 1943 when he presented a report suggesting centralisation development to Durham County Council. He felt that centralisation of services such as housing and shopping was the way forward and could be achieved by providing a new town for the Easington District. This would be much more cost-effective, allowing investment in a whole new town providing shared facilities without the need to provide them in individual villages.

In his 1946 report, 'Farewell Squalor', Mr Clarke wrote that the miners 'lacked cultural, recreational and shopping facilities alongside their inadequate living conditions' and that individual villages were unsuitable for expansion. He felt that the planning of a bigger project that would provide these amenities was the best way forward, at the same time reassuring residents of the traditional colliery villages that their villages would not be abandoned.

Farewell squalor.

In planning for the building of the new town that would lead to massive changes in the colliery villages within the Easington District, it would appear that there were a large amount of people involved in the decision making who, perhaps for the first time, seemed to be taking into account the needs of women married to coal miners in their plans. People like Lewis Silkin, the Government Minister for Town and Country Planning, Mr Clarke, the Chief Engineer and Surveyor for Easington District Council, Dr Monica Felton, the first Chair of the Development Corporation, architect Berthold Lubetkin and even the National Coal Board, all had the role of women in mind when considering plans for the new town.

The new town offered a major change to living conditions and lifestyle and was a massive challenge to the long-standing, familiar routines of the mining families who saw their villages as close-knit communities, where community spirit, camaraderie, a sense of belonging and the support of your neighbours was valued and could be relied upon. They found it difficult to imagine a situation that would involve leaving extended family and their social networks behind. Families relied upon and provided support to one another, support that would be lost by moving to the new town. However, we also know that, during the time when the miners operated under the hated bond system (abolished in 1872), families moved regularly as they searched for the elusive better deal out of life in the coal mining areas. Conversely though, the families at that time were moving to where the work and therefore housing was – not, as in this instance, away from their jobs to live in a new area, and to travel back to the village they had come from for their work.

Living in Wheatley Hill and similar areas, in poor-quality, rent-free accommodation provided by the coal board was a small price to pay for some, who felt the benefits of colliery village life outweighed the disadvantages of their living arrangements. Council-built accommodation was available, away from the pithead in most villages, but many felt that their rents were too high and while some may have been tempted by the facilities and housing provided by new town living, the even higher rents made it very unattractive to others. They accepted that there was some poor housing in their own village but felt that they had good facilities for shopping and recreation, and many felt a new town in the area would lead to neglect and deterioration of village life together with a lack of future development in individual villages.

Despite opposition from a great many people and organisations, the new town went ahead and was named after miners' leader and ex county councillor Peter Lee, who had strong connections with the village of Wheatley Hill and the Easington District. He was (and still is) regarded as a hero in recognising the changes that needed to be made in order to improve the quality of life of coal mining families at the beginning of the 1900s, concentrating on providing a system of clean drinking water for the colliery villages. C.W. Clarke's author's notes at the end of the 'Farewell Squalor' document sums up the man who would have a town named after him:

I have come to the conclusion that this new town should bear the name of some local man who, during this lifetime, went fearlessly and courageously forward for the good and uplift of the people in this district. A man who was a power both in bodily physique and mental ability and whose statue would grace the town square, a man who had the courage of his own convictions – and there are few of these, a man whose very presence commanded respect and attention, a man who, had he lived today, would have supported this project whole heartedly, knowing full well that it will be a town for social and individual living, containing healthy and pleasant living conditions, facilities for education, recreation, pleasure and social intercourse, provided near to the homes so that they may be enjoyed to the full, as a normal happening of everyday life and without being regarded as a luxury to be sought for in other places. Having all these virtues in one single frame seems well-nigh impossible. I am convinced, however that there was one person whose life was moulded on these virtues and whose memory could be appropriately perpetuated by the naming of the new town – PETERLEE.

No jerry builders will be permitted in Peterlee. The scum of the building trades will not be allowed to stake a claim in this new town of ours. Their nefarious operations have been permitted long enough. Peterlee must be designed in all its phases by a modern and proven team of impartial experts and only the best is good enough.

Let us therefore, close our eyes on the nineteenth century degradation and squalor, and let us only look with unseeing eyes on the sordid excrescence of the first decade of this century, let us blind ourselves to the septic and ugly building wens and ribbons perpetrated and planted on us between the wars, but let us open our eyes and look brightly forward and onward to the new town, the new living ... Peterlee.

Taking Mr Clarke's comments into account, it is interesting that we learn from the unpublished memoirs of Thornley councillor and miners' leader Hubert Tunney, who worked closely with Peter Lee during the 1920s, that when a centralised housing scheme was suggested at the end of the First World War to provide new houses for the villages of Wheatley Hill, Thornley, Shotton and Haswell at a site on

Peter Lee.

Haswell Moor near Shotton Colliery, Lee, when consulted as the chairman of Wingate Parish Council to which Wheatley Hill belonged, said he didn't agree with the centralised scheme. He said that if new houses were to be built for the people of Wheatley Hill, they would be built in their own village. It is likely, therefore, had he been alive, that Peter Lee may have objected to the new town in the 1940s as the parish councils of the affected villages did.

It is also interesting that Peterlee didn't get the statue of Peter Lee, or even a town square mentioned in C.W. Clarke's notes (above).

The new towns were controlled by development corporations and not the local or county councils in the area where they were built. The development corporations were financed by the government and given powers of compulsory purchase and planning, bypassing the local authority. They also had responsibility for the design and management of the new towns.

The National Coal Board and the Labour Party throughout the Easington District, supported by their MP, Manny Shinwell, and the miners' union, were very much opposed to the building of the new town. Living in the village in which they were also employed was convenient and had been a way of life for coal miners for generations. If a miner changed his job and moved to another pit, he was allocated accommodation in that pit village, so that at any time of the day or night he was available to get to and from work. The men recognised that if the same jobs were to be maintained from the new town, then consideration would have to be given to transportation, which could prove logistically difficult given the shift patterns, and may add considerably more time onto their working day.

Durham County Council, in supporting the new town and recognising opposition from all sides, decided that once Peterlee became a community they would only permit limited housing development in the east Durham villages, and use their funding for housing in the new town. To make sure there was no misunderstanding of their intentions, in their Development Plan of 1951 the county council categorised the villages of the Easington District and Peterlee 'A' to 'D':

Category 'A' – Peterlee – where development would be encouraged and permitted
Category 'C' – colliery villages – where not much, if any, new developments would be allowed (Wheatley Hill was in this category)
Category 'D' – no economic assistance given to these villages

The National Coal Board was very much opposed to the new town. It warned that the development of land heavily mined and therefore liable to subsidence would restrict further coal extraction in the area. The NCB suggested low-rise buildings be a feature of the new town in order to avoid the subsidence risk. Their continued objections and suggestions considerably slowed down the initial development of the new town and was responsible in the beginning for its piecemeal development as planners had to take into account their demands for the right to extract coal.

In 1956 the concerns of Thornley residents were raised in a parish council meeting. These concerns surrounded figures produced by Durham County Council about the proposed slum clearance programme at Thornley that would affect 1,700 people and the council only had plans to provide accommodation for 900, the rest to be housed at Peterlee, in line with their Category C status. The chair of the Parish Council, planning to contact Durham County Council, said, 'Our people do not want to go to Peterlee.' These concerns were still being raised in 1959 and 1960, when there were further protests from colliery villages that their residents didn't want to relocate to the new town but wanted council-built housing in their villages.

The new town was offering so much more than new housing opportunities for mining families. It offered them new ways in which to organise their working arrangements and family life in a more independent way, and it offered massive changes in lifestyle and working. However, these were changes many mining families didn't want to accept as they didn't see them as being 'for the best'.

However, in 1952 the Durham Miners Association and individual mining lodges withdrew their support of the NCB's objection to the new town due to the increased likelihood of pit closures over the next few years, and they felt it would be prudent for new industry to be attracted to the area and made available in the new town to provide jobs for men and women in the event of future job losses in the pits.

The Greenhills seam at Wheatley Hill pit closed in 1953 and in 1959 talks were underway concerning the uncertainty of a coal industry that was facing a recession in world trade, the growth of overseas competition and fierce competition from other sources of power such as oil, nuclear energy and natural gas. Coal exports were down while the figures for coal imports had risen significantly by 1959.

The development of the new town was slow and by 1957 the facilities on offer to the residents were an Anglican church followed in 1958 by a Methodist church. In 1960 the health centre opened and in 1962 the library. Despite the slow provision of amenities, the population grew significantly from 5,000 in 1955 to 12,000 in 1960 at the time of the visit of Queen Elizabeth II and the Duke of Edinburgh.

The new town was nicknamed 'Baby Town' by the *Daily Express* in 1961 as one third of the population was under the age of 10 years old, which suggested that it was mainly young people from the colliery villages supporting the facilities and a new way of living.

Eden Hill and Thorntree Gill were the first areas to be developed and in the early days of the town, the colliery villages probably had more to offer in terms of facilities than Peterlee did. Early settlers in the new town had very few shops, a limited bus service that restricted their access to extended family still living in the colliery villages who would have assisted with childcare, high rents and no nurseries for their children. In addition, the original plan for the new town to provide centralised and substantial facilities that could be enjoyed by the surrounding villages took a while to materialise as the colliery villages continued to enjoy the advantages of community living. However, the new residents felt that their new housing, healthy air, absence of squalor, peace and quiet and no sign of heavy industry more than made up for their high rents, lack of shopping, entertainment or churches and the lack of a bus service to other parts of the area apart from Horden.

Putting the coal in at Peterlee, 1958.

Retailers and manufacturers were slow to respond to the opportunities available to them in the new development area at Peterlee. They felt it was a high-risk investment due to a poor road network that would limit the transportation of goods. The A19 that served Peterlee was narrow and winding and capable of accomodating only slow-moving vehicles, and its lack of a rail station added to the disadvantages for transporting goods into the town. Shops in the shopping area mostly stood empty, with only ten out of twenty occupied by the early 1960s. Woolworth was the first retailer to set up in the main shopping street, with potential retailers looking on with interest to see if it would be successful before making a move.

The provision of female employment started in 1955 when Bradford-based textile spinners Jeremiah Ambler opened a factory in the town, followed in 1956 by Alexandre, a Leeds clothing manufacturer, and by 1958 these two factories were providing employment for 600 women and 100 men. In 1960 Tudor Foods opened a factory, which became the town's largest single employer, predominantly of female labour, and offered the advantage of shift work to married women who could plan their work around their care-giving duties. The opportunity to work at Tudor was taken up by many women from the surrounding colliery villages, the shift work being a major factor in their choice. Most women at this time wanted to add to the family budget and, if they lived in Peterlee, help with the high rent, by working at a job that would fit in with the needs of their husbands and children while not looking for a career.

7

ELIZABETH (BETTY) UNSWORTH

The colliery villages provided excellent facilities for young people socialising, both during and after the Second World War. Wheatley Hill had the Embassy Ballroom in the front street and regular dances were held at the Miners' Welfare Hall. The village also had two cinemas, the Regal and the Royalty, and most neighbouring villages had similar facilities, of which both Alf and Gordon took advantage.

It was at the Embassy Ballroom in 1947 that Gordon met his first serious girlfriend, Betty Unsworth, a shop assistant from Wingate. Betty was attending the dance with her friend Enid Proudlock, and after a few weeks of meeting up there, Gordon and Betty started seeing each other on nights other than dance night. A favourite pastime on a summer evening for young couples who didn't have much money during the 1940s was a walk up and down the Slack Bank between the Fir Tree, Wingate and Thornley Crossings. This route was very busy with courting couples as it was convenient if one lived at Wingate and the other at either the bottom end of Wheatley Hill or Shotton. Alternatively, a popular walk for courting couples from the top end of the village was along the Durham Road, while the road between Wheatley Hill and the Halfway House was known as 'Lovers' Lane'.

Betty was born at Wingate in 1930, the youngest of the four children of coal miner Jim Unsworth and his wife Bella. She was brought up in the Roman Catholic faith, her father being a Roman Catholic and her mother a Methodist. They lived at No. 30 Market Crescent, one of the new council-built houses at Wingate, having moved there from their colliery house at Pickering Street. Jim was a coal miner but made no secret of the fact that he didn't like to go to work. He much preferred to spend his time reading books borrowed from the library, watching the television in the Wingate workingmen's club or socialising at the Green Door (the Wingate Catholic Club). He blamed his lack of motivation for work on an injury he received during the Second World War when he was stationed in Northern Ireland as part of the Military Police. He was never specific about the injury, but it involved a hospital stay in the Holywood Military Hospital near Belfast. Apart from spending some time in Ireland, he was also part of the British Expeditionary Force evacuated from Dunkirk. I have since read the remarks on his release papers from the Army in 1945, and they describe him as 'Military conduct exemplary – a reliable man and a conscientious worker, sober and honest'.

I am not sure my grandma would agree with the Army description of her husband for as a result of his poor motivation for work she had to take on various cleaning jobs in order to make up for the unreliable wages he brought home and she always carried her purse in her pinny pocket, which suggested that the money she earned was hers and not to be shared with him. My Wingate grandma was known to everyone as Bella. She was a blunt speaker and could be relied upon to always tell you the truth with little or no regard for finer feelings. You always knew what she was thinking because she told you! When addressing her grandchildren she went through a range of names, so when she was speaking to me she would say, 'Jean, Carol, Margaret', the names of all of her granddaughters, and the same with the boys. Her father, Kit Napier, and Jim's mother, Bess Unsworth, lived with the family while Betty and her siblings were growing up and Jim's large family were frequent visitors to their home, visiting their mother/grandmother, and Betty remembered it as a very busy, happy home. Most of the

Unsworths were musical and were described as good singers, and Jim's nephew, Jacky Cain from Wheatley Hill, a well-known musician in the colliery villages, often visited his grandmother at Market Crescent and would sing and play to entertain the family on Bella and Jim's piano.

Betty and her siblings all attended St Mary's Roman Catholic school, which was adjacent to the welfare park at Wingate, and they also went to St Peter and St Paul's Church at Hutton Henry, being taken there by their father twice on a Sunday as they walked from Wingate, a round trip of about 4 miles, whatever the weather. Betty was confirmed there in 1942.

As they were growing up, Betty and her sisters didn't confine themselves to one religion and attended services at the Wingate Salvation Army or any of the chapels, particularly if they were putting on entertainment such as parties or pantomimes. The girls were encouraged in this by their mother, who was very critical of the Roman Catholic faith, refusing to 'turn' when she married Jim in 1923 at the Easington Registry Office. That did not go down well with his family at all, and she was reluctant to agree to allow the children to be brought up as Roman Catholic but was overruled. There was only so much aggravation Jim could stand from his sisters.

Betty was outgoing and confident, and being the youngest of the four children probably had more access to planned activities outside of the home while she was growing up than her siblings. She had regular piano and dancing lessons and she especially loved the performing aspect of dancing.

While she enjoyed her time at school, Betty's enjoyment wasn't related to learning. She loved helping the teachers out with a variety of tasks and was popular with the staff, including the nuns. She walked to school most days with the head teacher, Mr Reed, and his son Nicholas, as they passed through Market Crescent from their home in Dobson Terrace. Nicholas was the same age as Betty and they were often busy in the school garden well before the other children arrived, but Betty knew she hadn't achieved as she should and felt she would be better suited to the workplace and couldn't wait to leave school. She was delighted therefore when, in 1944 after leaving school on a Friday in July, she obtained employment as a shop assistant with

Walter Willsons Grocery Store, Wingate front street.

Walter Willson's grocery store situated at the bottom of Wingate front street, starting on the following Monday morning.

Employment suited her much better than her education had, and she quickly settled into the junior role, which involved her in delivering groceries around the village and further afield on a tradesman's delivery bike with a basket on the front. Her deliveries took her to the outlying areas of Castle Eden, Hutton Henry and the farms of Naisbitt and Hulam, near Sheraton. Betty undertook all tasks related to the shop with enthusiasm and quickly adapted to writing down and adding up a customer order quickly and accurately. All groceries were loose and delivered to the shops in barrels, crates or tea chests. Betty learned to pat the butter into blocks of different sizes, weighing them on big brass scales, then wrapping them in greaseproof paper before the packages were transferred into strong dark paper packets and handed to the customer. The advertising slogan for Walter Willson shops was 'A Smiling Service' and Betty provided this, becoming a popular member of staff with the customers as well as the shop manager, Connie Brown, and they remained firm friends for the rest of their lives.

Betty and Enid (middle centre) on the Wingate trip to Blackpool.

When she was 17, Betty went on holiday for the first time with her friend Enid and Enid's parents, Mr and Mrs Proudlock. They went on a coach trip from Wingate to Blackpool and the girls were so excited to be spending time at the seaside. They were able to explore Blackpool on their own and loved the sandy beaches, the pleasure park and dancing in the evenings. Blackpool was described in the resort brochure in 1947 as: 'The Holiday Playground of the World, offering a large range of accommodation to suit all pockets'. After this first trip, Betty became a regular visitor to the resort with her friends, joining the many bus trips leaving Wingate during the summer months.

As her relationship with Gordon progressed, she became a regular visitor to Gowland Terrace and it was clear that Gordon's parents liked her and were careful not to mention her Roman Catholicism. Gordon was also popular with Bella and Jim at Wingate. They didn't have any objection to Betty seeing a boy who wasn't a Roman Catholic – Betty felt that this was because her mother wasn't Catholic and made all the decisions anyway, and her father was very easygoing and wanted his children to be happy.

They made a striking couple. Betty was a very attractive young woman and Gordon a good-looking young man, and the relationship between them continued to grow. In 1948 Betty was invited to go on holiday with Gordon and his parents. Her family weren't in a position to have annual holidays and apart from Blackpool Betty hadn't travelled anywhere else. Billy had changed his car by 1948 and now had a Humber 16, which was powerful enough to tow a caravan, so they hired one and toured around Scotland for two weeks. Billy kept a diary of the holiday and notes that over the fourteen days they travelled 697 miles. On 29 July 1952 he recorded that they visited Fort William, and that Gordon and Betty attempted a walk up Ben Nevis. He completes his fourteen-day commentary with the words, 'we had a good trip from start to finish'.

It was at the end of 1952 that Betty realised she was pregnant. She visited her GP, Dr Jackson, who confirmed it, and she told Gordon before she told her mother. He was 24 and Betty 22. There was an understanding between them that they would marry, but they hadn't got around to arranging anything or becoming engaged. However, with a baby due in the summer of 1953, they were forced into action.

Neither was looking forward to telling their parents, but they realised it had to be done. Gordon had no idea how his parents would react. Things such as this were never discussed in his family. He knew that his mother and his aunt from Ludworth talked about 'private' things, but whenever he (or anyone else) approached them, they stopped. His brother Alf was already married. He had left his job at Wheatley Hill pit after serving his apprenticeship as an electrician, and as a result of his success in his Higher National Certificate, obtained employment at the Reyrolle engineering company based at Hebburn on Tyneside. He and his wife, Nancy, bought a house in Argyle Street and settled well into their new surroundings. Gordon was proud of his brother's achievements and knew that their parents were too, so he didn't know how this news would go down. Gordon had completed his apprenticeship at the pit and now worked there as a mechanical fitter. While he was good at his job, he didn't have the ambition of his older brother, especially with regard to furthering his education, but had managed to persevere to pass his senior course in general engineering. Their parents never compared the two boys, but Gordon knew that his lack of ambition must have frustrated them and would have been discussed privately between them, and now it was him that had got a girl pregnant.

They decided that they would tell Betty's mother first. When they discussed how their parents might react, Betty felt her mother would be realistic about what she was being told and practical in the advice she gave. Gordon couldn't begin to think what his parents might say, and he was happy to put off the inevitable as long as possible. When he arrived at Market Crescent he was as nervous as he'd ever been in his life. He had never discussed anything so private and personal with anyone and he hardly knew Mrs Unsworth and hoped that Betty would do the talking. She was waiting outside to try and reassure him, and to tell him that her da wasn't in. Gordon felt some relief at hearing that, but Jim Unsworth would have laughed had he known that Gordon was frightened to face him with the pregnancy news. Jim was very laid back and took everything in his stride. Betty was his youngest daughter, and he wouldn't have done or said anything to upset her, whatever the circumstances.

The meeting with Betty's mother went well, better than Gordon could have expected, but with Betty doing the talking. Bella told them that she and Jim wouldn't be able to afford a big wedding but would give them the best send-off they could. She said, 'And don't go getting married in St Peter's and Paul's mind.'

'We haven't given that any thought, ma,' said Betty.

'Well just don't that's all. Gordon's not a Catholic and if you get married there, they'll mak ye bring ye bairns up Catholic and he won't get a say in it. So, think on. Our Winny didn't get married there so it can be done, even though yer da's family will be put out. Have ye told yer own ma, lad?' Winny was Betty's older sister who had also married outside of the Catholic faith and Betty knew that their Aunt Lizzie had had a lot to say to her da about it.

'No not yet Mrs Unsworth, we thought we'd tell you first, so when we leave here, we'll go straight to Wheatley Hill to tell them.'

Bella said she would tell Jim the news when he came in.

'And dinnit look so worried lad, there's worse things that can happen than havin' a bairn ye know'. Gordon wasn't so sure and couldn't think of anything worse at the time, apart from having to talk to his parents about it.

Aunt Lizzie Cain was one of Jim Unsworth's elder sisters who lived at Wheatley Hill. She was a staunch Roman Catholic and very critical of those who married outside the faith. When she got to know that Betty was courting Gordon she had made a special visit to Market Crescent to tell her brother that he had to put a stop to it. Jim wasn't very brave where his sister was concerned. He listened but didn't promise anything and had no intention of doing anything, despite the arguments their Lizzie was putting forward. He felt it best to be non-committal or she would have the rest of his sisters, all seven of them, on his doorstep, so it was best to let her think he was taking her comments into consideration.

The two young people hurried out of the house, relieved that the ordeal was over. Gordon had felt most uncomfortable talking to Betty's mother about an unplanned pregnancy and had said as little as possible. He thought Mrs Unsworth had taken the news well but was sure his own mother wouldn't be so understanding. The only thing in their favour was that both his parents liked Betty.

When they arrived at Gowland Terrace, Bella and Billy thought nothing of Betty being with Gordon in the middle of the week, as she was a regular visitor to their home, but Gordon was expecting a more difficult conversation than the one they had with Mrs Unsworth and knew he would have to take the lead this time.

'We've been to Wingate to see Betty's parents,' he said.

'Oh?' Bella replied.

'Aye, we went to tell them that Betty's expecting a bairn,' Gordon said, realising too late that he could have been a bit more tactful.

'A bairn, by that's a shock, when?'

'In the summer, so we're ganna to get married.'

'And aah should hope so too,' Bella said, in her telling off voice.

'What do you think, da?' Gordon quickly asked his father before things escalated with his mother.

'Why what can aah think? What's done's done and aah always thowt ye'd be getting married anyway.'

'Aye, why that's true,' Gordon said, 'We didn't plan to do it this way, but it has given us the push we needed to get married.'

'Well, that's that then,' Billy said, 'Bella aah think we have a wedding to plan for.'

Gordon was grateful for his da taking charge of the conversation, knowing he had done so to stop his ma having her say, but no doubt she would have it in private with his da, or worse still with him when Betty had gone home.

'Me ma and da will give us a wedding,' Betty said, 'it'll be quiet but it would have been anyway.' Betty was aware of the difference in financial circumstances between Mr and Mrs Carr and her own parents, and was anxious to let them know that she and Gordon were not relying on them to pay for the wedding.

'We'll help out where we can,' Bella said, her genuine liking for Betty reducing her disappointment of the situation a little. 'Just let us know what we can do. Where will you get married, in the Catholic Church?'

'We hadn't thought about it until me ma said we shouldn't,' Betty said, 'so we'll talk about it and decide where it should be.'

Out of wedlock pregnancies were common and both Bella and Billy knew of friends and family who had married as a result of one. Of course, in true Victorian tradition and as a result of her strict upbringing, this sort of thing was never discussed openly by Bella, particularly with her sons, although she had surprised son Alf when he told his parents he was applying for a special licence to marry his girlfriend, Nancy Wigham from Thornley.

'Do you have to get married?' Bella asked, the implication being clear.

'No of course not,' Alf replied, 'but if I'm going to live in Hebburn, we thought we should get married sooner rather than later that's all and a special licence is quicker because you don't have to wait for the Banns to be called.'

'Oh well, that's very sensible,' Bella replied. Conversation over.

Family group at wedding, 1953.

As she got older, Betty realised she wasn't such a regular practising Catholic as she had been when she was younger and, particularly after leaving the Catholic school at Wingate, her church attendance had just been Easter duties and Christmas once she started work. Gordon wasn't religious but had attended the Wesleyan Methodist Chapel at the bottom of Church Street mainly because his friends went there, and the chapel provided a good social life. So, discussing a place to get married wasn't connected to either of their affiliations to a particular religion, but both agreed that they would prefer a church service to a registry office wedding, and decided they would approach the vicar at the Anglican church of Holy Trinity, Wingate, in order to hold the wedding ceremony there.

The wedding was held on 14 March 1953, the day after Betty's 23rd birthday, with only family present. Betty's family consisted of her parents, two sisters, their husbands and children and her brother and his wife. Gordon's parents, his brother Alf and sister-in-law Nancy and Gordon's cousin Norman Grainger made up the wedding party. Alf was Gordon's best man and Nancy, Betty's matron of honour. The small reception was held at No. 30 Market Crescent with the food supplied by Robinsons butchers of Wingate and Duncans grocery store. The usual wedding reception food was on offer: ham and pease pudding, pickles, bread buns and fresh cream cakes. Betty's friend and colleague from Walter Willson's, Connie Brown, made them a cake as her wedding gift and there was a bottle of sherry and a bottle of whisky to toast the happy couple.

Billy and Bella paid for a photographer to be present to make a record of the occasion and they made a handsome couple on their special day. Gordon wore his best suit and Betty a blue two-piece with matching hat from Doggarts Department Store.

Gordon and Betty's wedding, 1953.

Most people employed at the pit, as Gordon was, would be moving into a colliery-owned house in the village after they married and then put their names down for a council house at the other end of the village, and had it not been for his brother Alf taking the major step of buying a house, Gordon and Betty probably would have done the same. However, house ownership was becoming more popular, and Alf advised his brother that it was a good investment for the future as they would never see any return on payments made on rental properties.

There wasn't much privately owned housing in Wheatley Hill, but Gordon became aware of a house at No. 6 Lynn Terrace that might be for sale. The house had been owned by Mr Cook, a foreman joiner at the pit, and following his death his wife's health had deteriorated to such an extent that she moved in with her sister at Wingate, leaving the house empty for quite some time. Betty's mother knew Mrs Cook's sister and arranged for them to visit Mrs Cook, who agreed to sell them the house for £550. Between them they were able to raise the £100 deposit needed to secure the sale and after speaking to the colliery engineer, who was one of the directors of the Thornley and District Building Society, a mortgage was arranged for the rest of the payment over a twenty-five-year period.

No. 6 Lynn Terrace (first on right), Wheatley Hill.

The Lynn Terrace houses were built during the 1880s and the street at first consisted of twelve houses that were added to later to include a further thirteen houses. They were the only houses in Wheatley Hill at the time to be administered under Shadforth Parish and Durham County Council, the rest of the village coming under the administration of Wingate Parish and Easington District Council, Gore Burn being the dividing line that gave the street the description of 'over the beck'. The houses were built alongside the Moon's Hotel (which later became the Colliery Hotel) and the street got its name from the landlord of the pub, John Lynn, who died in 1890 just at the time the houses were being completed.

The houses were of the terraced type, built solidly of red brick. The front door opened onto a lobby and passageway with two doors leading off to the sitting room and the living room. There was also a scullery downstairs while upstairs there were two bedrooms. Outside facilities included a back yard that contained an ash closet toilet, wash house and coal store. The houses also had a substantial garden on land across the back street.

Gowland Terrace was a short walk away and could be reached by a footbridge over the beck, up the black path past the allotments.

When they went to view the property, they found that at some point after Mrs Cook had moved out the house had suffered flooding from the only tap in the property, which had been dripping in the kitchen. As there wasn't a sink, the tap was dripping into an enamel bowl, which eventually overflowed. It wasn't a very good start to home ownership, but Gordon had the skills to carry out the repair and make improvements as far as the plumbing was concerned, and Betty and his mother worked hard to make the rooms habitable and attractive through their thorough cleaning and decorating.

Before moving into the property, Gordon was able to fit a porcelain sink in the scullery together with a tap for cold water and added an Ascot boiler run by Calor Gas to provide hot water. Another improvement carried out to the property by Gordon and his father was the laying of a concrete floor in the living room, the original floor being badly damaged by the flood while the house stood empty.

They worked hard during the beginning of 1953 to make their house into a home but took a day off on the day of the Coronation of Queen Elizabeth II, which took place on Saturday, 2 June. Wheatley Hill, along with the other colliery villages in the Easington District, had a full programme of events planned for the celebration. However, many of these were spoilt by the poor weather conditions on the day. Betty and Gordon watched the Coronation on Billy and Bella's new HMV television set bought especially for the occasion from Perry's of Hartlepool. It was in a walnut case and the screen measured 12 inches. Bella had a houseful on that day, including Meggie, Billy's mother, Mrs Smith from next door and Mr and Mrs Craig, who also lived in Gowland Terrace. They all sat round the small screen, marvelling at events that were happening in London in the rain. A flexible and coloured piece of Perspex that came with the television was held in front of the screen at different times throughout the day. It was coloured green at the bottom and blue at the top to give the impression of grass and sky, but it didn't always seem to fit with what was on the screen at the time.

The only downside to the celebrations, but only to Billy, was that his local pub, the Colliery Hotel in Lynn Terrace, had closed and its licence transferred to a new pub to be built near the store that would be called the Coronation.

8

A NEW ARRIVAL

And that's how I joined my family story. Margaret Carr, born 8 p.m. on Saturday, 8 August 1953 at the Grantully Nursing Home, Westbourne Road, Hartlepool. One of the first generation of children to be born outside of the home in an establishment supported by the new National Health Service and into a generation that would represent 'the last women of the Durham coalfield'. The National Health Service changed women's lives for the better, particularly women having babies. Before its creation, babies of the working classes continued to be born at home and during the 1950s hospital births increased, although women laboured without a birth partner as dads were not present at the birth, something that my dad was very relieved about. Grantully was run by doctors and midwives for women with a history of uncomplicated births and with the expectation of a normal delivery.

There was a slum clearance scheme underway when I was born in the area of Lynn Terrace where the colliery houses built in the 1860s were being demolished and the residents were relocating to the new council houses at the other end of the village away from the pit. Wheatley Hill pit was in trouble and the Greenhills seam closed in 1953. Despite this I was, apparently, born into a period that saw the development of

Left: Grantully Nursing Home, Hartlepool. Right: Margaret Carr, born August 1953.

'the affluent society' with full employment, social security and economic growth. Britain at the time I was born was becoming a consumer society in which people wanted their children to do better than the previous generation had.

I became the newest member of a very close-knit family unit that included my paternal grandparents, who lived near us. I was their eldest grandchild. My uncle Alf's daughter, Hilary, was born in October of the same year. I was baptised at the Anglican Church of All Saints, Wheatley Hill, on Sunday, 30 August 1953 by the Rev. Arthur Preston, and that was where my regular church-going, including confirmation, was established and continued well into my teenage years. My Godparents were my grandma, uncle Alf and aunty Nancy.

My feeling of belonging extended into the Lynn Terrace community, which was isolated from the rest of the village and where everyone knew everyone else. This was the same for all areas of a pit village though, and as a child growing up there, I knew that if I stepped out of line away from my own home any of the neighbours would tell me off. This was expected by all children and their parents, and it certainly made me think twice about misbehaving outside the home as I knew my mam would get to know, would want to know and would let me know that she knew!

Most of my preschool time was spent with my mam in Lynn Terrace or my grandma in Gowland Terrace, a short walk across the beck footbridge, a journey I could make on my own from an early age. The first time was when I escaped from the house without my mam's knowledge aged about 3 years old. By the time she realised I had gone, I was crossing the footbridge over the beck. She followed to see where I would go, and I walked up the black path straight to the gate of my grandma's house.

We visited my Wingate grandma and granda once a week on a Friday, travelling by bus from the colliery office bus stop. They were used to grandchildren as they already had three, but welcomed the weekly visits of me and my mam. One of the highlights of my visits to my Wingate grandma's was going to the house of her next-door neighbour, Meggie Chatt, either for pop or vinegar. Meggie Chatt was a little old lady, always dressed in black. She never had much to say to me but provided dandelion and burdock, ice cream soda and other flavours of fizzy pop from her kitchen. As a child I was really impressed by the funnel she used to pour vinegar from a very big bottle into small bottles and longed to have one of my own! She was obviously an agent for a drinks company, but I didn't realise that at the time, and in my childish reasoning I just thought it was really convenient to have such a useful next-door neighbour. It was years later that I realised Meggie's name was Mrs Chapman and I hoped that I hadn't addressed her as Mrs Chatt during my many visits to her home.

Our neighbours in Lynn Terrace were Mr Goyns in No. 5 and Mr and Mrs Marshall at No. 7. Mr Goyns was a very quiet and hard of hearing elderly man who kept himself to himself. He kept hens in his garden across the back street and that was the only time we saw him as he went to feed them, apart from a Thursday afternoon when he left his home to visit the Post Office in the front street to collect his pension. He listened to *The Archers* on his radio at 7 p.m. every night and we heard the theme tune through our wall.

Mr and Mrs Marshall had the only front door in the street to be protected with a big striped curtain, a bit like a deckchair. They too were elderly and very staunch supporters of the Anglican church in Wheatley Hill. Mr Marshall was a church warden and they both attended church regularly as well as other organisations associated with the church such as the Mother's Union and the Over 20s Club. When introducing my mam to our new vicar, Mr Graham, one day when he came to visit, Mrs Marshall said to him, 'Oh vicar you must meet my neighbour, Mrs Carr, she's an RC lady, but ever so nice.' The vicar and my mam just smiled as they shook hands. Mr Marshall worked at the pit as a traffic manager and Mrs Marshall was a very good dressmaker and on two memorable occasions called upon my dad's help with her tasks. She called upon my mam for help with many things, but dressmaking wasn't one of them.

The only time Mrs Marshall needed help with her dressmaking tasks was when she was making large items that were difficult to handle. During the 1960s she was engaged in making a whole new set of decorative altar frontals and matching pulpit hangings for All Saints Church to represent the different church seasons. It was a task that required extensive panel work and measuring to create complicated angles etc., and it was my dad that she turned to for help in creating a range of templates to work from. He wasn't sure what his role would be in providing help or how he had been recruited, but very reluctantly made himself available after much discussion between him and my mam!

The damask being used was of high quality and expensive, and therefore it was vitally important that errors be avoided at all costs. In putting into perspective why Mrs Marshall should think that my dad was suitable to provide help, she will have known from her brother, Jack Richardson, my dad's boss at the pit and the foreman fitter, that the fitters and blacksmiths at Wheatley Hill pit were considered to provide excellent service to the colliery. They rarely ordered parts for machinery as they manufactured their own and their skills were well known throughout the district. As a result of their efficiency, the stores at Wheatley Hill pit carried the minimum amount of spare parts, so when she needed help with measuring or cutting she turned to someone with precision engineering skills who, she felt, could transfer his abilities to the accurate measurement and cutting of damask. It was something that definitely didn't appear on his senior engineering course, and I can remember both of them being involved in long discussions about the best way to tackle the complicated designs on all four sets of the altar cloths and my dad providing templates made out of brown paper.

One of her other memorable tasks was making me a multi-layered dress to wear for ballroom dancing competitions. This was probably a first for her as I don't believe she will have had much call for dresses of this type before I joined a ballroom dancing class in the early 1960s. The 'team' of Mrs Marshall and my dad spent time discussing the best way to make the dress and when they had decided, my dad produced the template or pattern with brown paper and I can remember him cutting out lots of circles of pink net, each with a hole in the middle where I would fit and where the bodice would be attached. It was a work of art, and although I danced the part of the boy with my friend Pauline, we were successful in several competitions in our net ballroom dancing dresses.

Even as a young child I loved the routine of life in Lynn Terrace and Gowland Terrace. I knew the days when the storeman was coming to take the order and leave the milk checks to put in our bottle so that Sammy the milkman would know how much milk we wanted. I knew the days the meat and green grocery was delivered, all by horse and cart. The delivery drivers were known by everyone in the village and Norman Carr, my dad's cousin, brought the green grocery on a Thursday. The delivery men lived in Wheatley Hill, and it was another example of a close-knit community in a colliery village. I looked forward to a chat with Jane the postwoman at both Lynn Terrace and Gowland Terrace, often on the same day as I travelled between both houses.

During my formative years, I suppose I realised that things were done differently by my mam and my grandma. My grandma still followed her strict housekeeping routines that she had been brought up with and that now, even in her 50s, were still important to her, whereas my mam had a more flexible approach to housekeeping. She still had routines, but they weren't as rigid as those supported by my grandma. My mam's household tasks were carried out according to need, and my grandma's were done as part of the long-held routine, whether or not they needed doing. My grandma never sat down with idle hands. When she watched the television on an evening, she always had some sort of mending to do or the crossword from the newspaper, and during the day, despite her housework, also found time for gardening. Apart from the newspaper, my grandma wasn't a reader, whereas my mam enjoyed her weekly magazine *Woman* and books borrowed from the library.

In the summer of 1955, aged only 2 years old, I was taken to see an old lady who I now know lived in Wordsworth Avenue near the store. It was a sunny day when me and my mam went with my grandma. We all went upstairs to the bedroom where a very old lady lay in a bed. She was smiling at me, and my grandma said, 'this is our Gordon's little lass' and the lady in the bed spoke to me and no doubt I answered her questions. I didn't realise until many years later that this was my great grandma, Meggie, and this was to be my only meeting with her as she died in 1955 and was buried in Wheatley Hill cemetery after a service in the chapel of rest on 13 August.

From an early age, I would often walk with my mam up to the front street, the main shopping street in the village, and it always surprised me when we changed direction really quickly, either by crossing the road or darting into a shop that we didn't normally go into. My mam's explanation on these occasions was, 'Oh no, here's Aunt Lizzie.' I didn't know who Aunt Lizzie was. She never visited our house, and we didn't visit hers, but she was clearly known (and feared) by my mam. When I was older and enquired about Aunt Lizzie, I found out that she was my Wingate granda's sister, a staunch Roman Catholic, who had objected most strongly about my mam marrying a 'proddy'. Even when this was explained to me, I still didn't see why it should be so important to avoid Aunt Lizzie, but my mam always assured me it was. This was my first realisation of the divide between the two religions, a divide we crossed regularly when we visited my Wingate grandparents without incident!

My granda, Billy Carr, was moved to another job in 1955. He was seconded onto the Coalface Mechanisation Team. This team of experienced mining engineers, senior colliery overmen, mechanical and electrical engineers were charged with overseeing the installation of specialised coalface machinery that mechanised the production of coal from coalfaces. This would replace the traditional manual hand-wrought and loaded methods with continuous mining using power-loading machines. As a result, the team were also tasked with supervising and leading the extensive retraining of miners to become power loaders on these new coalfaces. This mechanisation team in my granda's case operated in the Durham Coalfield No. 3 area. His new job involved travelling around the pits of Easington, Horden, Blackhall, Thornley, Shotton, Deaf Hill, Wheatley Hill and Wingate and he was part of that team until 1958. Interestingly, Wheatley Hill pit was never fully mechanised and so his home pit never had power-loading machines installed and remained dependent on traditional mining methods until it closed.

After his secondment, he became foreshift overman at Wheatley Hill pit. He was 55 at the time of taking up this appointment and his new role meant he was the man responsible for the Harvey district of the pit for the shift that went down at 3 a.m. He was also expected to spend time in the colliery office each afternoon between 4 p.m. and 5 p.m. to complete paperwork. He visited the pit on a Saturday morning, often taking me with him, to visit the lamp cabin. It was always warm, and I can still remember the oily smell and the rows of miners' lamps waiting to be taken down the pit. Along with his change of role came the opportunity for him and my grandma to move into a more prestigious colliery house – Auckland House, No. 3 Office Street. This is the house that was home to the colliery manager when the pit opened in 1869 but over the years, another house was built for the manager beside All Saints Church – Weardale House – and the Office Street property came to be occupied by under managers at the pit. The most recent was Fred Simpson, who had relocated to West House, Gable Terrace, another prestigious National Coal Board-owned house.

As the home of high-profile people within Wheatley Hill pit, Auckland House had suitably impressive facilities. It was at the end of a terrace of three houses, which I believe used to be four. The house was of large proportions both inside and out. The gardens on three sides were beautifully laid out and had been kept by

Auckland House, No. 3 Office Street, far left.

gardeners employed by the private coal owners and then the National Coal Board during the time of Mr Simpson and his predecessors. It had five lawns and was far too big for Bella and Billy, who would be looking after the garden without the services of a gardener. At the gate that overlooked the pit were a range of trees – four poplar, a laburnum next to the gate and a May tree in the corner near the coalhouse – and there was a flagpole on the lawn outside the back door. The outside of the house was well appointed with a wash house, outside flush toilet, coal store, tool store, three hen houses, a garage, summer house, greenhouse and potting shed. The orchard was planted with apple, plum and cherry trees. Through the gate leading to the main garden the upper terrace was laid out in three large flower beds, each with a rockery, and the bottom part of the garden towards the beck was planted with flowers and vegetables. Screening the different areas was achieved with the use of very attractive trellis with plants growing up it, and in the summer months no one ever left Billy Carr's garden without a range of garden produce including a bunch of flowers.

Billy and Bella in the summer house, No. 3 Office Street.

Unfortunately, I didn't ask my grandparents what it felt like to be living in such conditions, so far removed from those that they both grew up in at Ludworth and Wheatley Hill. I can only assume that it must have felt that they'd come a long way to be now living in eight-roomed accommodation with copious gardens after the poor-quality housing and lack of amenities of their childhoods. The house would provide a challenge to my grandma's home-making skills as her work-load would more than double with the extra rooms in this house and the garden would provide a challenge to both of them.

They loved gardening and were probably attracted to the house as a result of its garden that had been so well looked after. The house too was impressive compared with the rest of the colliery housing through-out the village. A large entrance hall led off to a staircase, scullery, kitchen, dining room, sitting room and a passageway leading to a front sitting room. Upstairs there were four double bedrooms and a walk-in cupboard, bathroom and separate toilet. Not having enough furniture of their own for all these rooms, they bought good second-hand items to fill the spaces up and it provided them with a very happy home.

One of the back bedrooms contained a tall set of mahogany drawers that had belonged to Susan, my grandma's mother. The drawers were a perfect fit in the large back bedroom in Office Street, but Bella wondered how her mother had managed to fit them into her living room in their Ludworth house and then into the Aged Miners Homes.

I loved the Office Street house. There were lots of places to play and hide both in the house and garden. I loved to help with picking and shelling the peas and laying them out on trays to dry in the sun in one of the back bedrooms facing the pit, picking strawberries when I shouldn't, collecting tomatoes from my granda's greenhouse. My grandma always made sure I never had idle hands either. If there weren't any food preparations to help with, she would sit me at the kitchen table with an old newspaper and pair of scissors to cut squares that she would hang on string in the outside toilet to supplement the horrible Izal waxy, disinfectant, prevention-against-infection toilet paper already in there.

Their next-door neighbours in Office Street were Mr and Mrs Beresford. Mr Beresford played in the colliery band, and I liked looking out for him when we saw the band playing at different events over the years. I think he played the cornet.

It is testament to the superior building materials used to build Office Street back in 1869 that the street exists today. The houses were built of red brick and apart from Gowland Terrace all other early colliery housing in Wheatley Hill was built of locally available limestone, which would be a cheaper building material and therefore appealing to the cost-cutting coal owners. The early streets were demolished during the 1950s and '60s along with other landmark buildings in the village such as the very attractive Haswell Co-operative Store opposite the Nimmo, built in the English Renaissance style, and the Sherburn Hill Store on Thornley Road. The Royalty Cinema, its frontage providing a fine example of art deco architecture, was sold to be used as a DIY store and later demolished, and the original Victorian school in the front street, opened in 1873, was also demolished, but not until the 1970s, along with its plaques containing names of its ex-pupils who lost their lives in the Second World War.

By the late 1950s my grandma still had a baking day once a week but she concentrated on pies and not the bread and cakes of previously, whereas my mam had a baking day very occasionally and made good use of the amount of convenience foods that became available after the war. We sometimes had a take-away meal of fish and chips from Hutchinson's fish shop in the front street, but this is something that my grandma and granda didn't do. We had baked beans, tinned spaghetti or tinned soup in our pantry, items that never appeared in my grandma's.

Like my grandma, my mam put an order in to the storeman on a Monday and it was delivered later in the week, but she bought bakery products on a Friday from Duncan's and Robinson's of Wingate while we were visiting my Wingate grandma and granda. It confused me when my Wingate grandma first sent me for 'tuffies' as I didn't know what they were, but realised they were what we called bread buns. As far as I knew, tuffies was not a term used in Wheatley Hill, but in Wingate it seemed everyone knew what they were. In the 1950s and '60s my Wheatley Hill grandma had a baker who delivered to her in the Office Street house on a Saturday morning; Taylor's Bakery would deliver brown bread, tea cakes and fancy cakes. Another delivery on a Friday afternoon was by Harrisons of Wingate, who delivered beer to my granda – ten bottles of Double Maxim. I was often present when these deliveries were made and can remember the beige van of the baker with 'Taylors' written along the side and the green van that seemed to have a lot of wood on the side that brought the beer from Harrisons. In Wheatley Hill we didn't have a Meggie Chatt, so we ordered our pop from Greys of Spennymoor, who delivered lemonade to my grandma and an assortment for us every two weeks on a Thursday.

My mam had been brought up through the rationing of the Second World War when ingredients were meagre and food to fill you up was the order of the day. My Wingate grandma was a good cook but due to lack of money and rationing, their meals were very basic. She hadn't been in a position to stockpile food items before the war but made the best use she could of rationed food. When we visited on a Friday, my mam usually took vegetables and salad stuff from my granda's garden.

We had tinned salmon sandwiches for special occasions and our salads in the summer consisted of leafy lettuce, tomatoes, scallions served with a boiled egg and usually cooked ham or tongue, and always bread and butter washed down by cups of tea. All our meals, except Sunday dinner, were finished off with a cup of tea and a piece of cake.

Our Sunday dinner was prepared very early in the morning and the vegetables put in a pan to boil for what seemed to be a very long time. They were always mushy by the time we came to eat them. My mam used to say that it took the oven ages to get hot on a Sunday because everyone else was using their ovens and there was a great demand for electricity. I didn't know whether or not that was true, but it was a regular topic of conversation between her and my grandma. On Sunday we had a dessert that was usually a fruit pie, usually rhubarb from my granda's garden or a milk pudding such as rice or sago. For Sunday tea we had tinned fruit and evaporated milk during the 1950s and early '60s, and it was always served with bread and butter.

I knew how both homes operated as I spent my time equally between my mam and my grandma and as a result of the adult stimulation was described as 'old fashioned'. I knew that's what the adults said about me, but I thought it must be a good thing as no one told me off for it.

9

MY MEMORIES
OF CHRISTMAS

The 1950s were a time before mass consumerism when children asked for only one main present and depending on family circumstances may also have been provided with smaller and cheaper items, including a Christmas stocking hung up on Christmas Eve that would be filled with maybe an orange, an apple, nuts and a three-penny or six-penny piece and perhaps a small toy. Along with my main gift, I always received an annual, which was usually *June* and then *June* and *School Friend*. *June* was also a weekly comic and featured a blonde schoolgirl who wore a red headband on the cover of the comic and the annuals.

In the weeks leading up to Christmas my mam and Wheatley Hill grandma would travel by the G&B bus to Bishop Auckland and the main branch of Doggarts Department Store. The Bishop Auckland store was in the marketplace, and before I started school I went along with them. It was a whole day out, and we had our dinner (at lunchtime) in Doggarts café before returning home to Wheatley Hill on the bus.

Doggarts department store, Wingate.

The Doggarts stores in general set up a big display of children's toys and at their Wingate store, which was near my Wingate grandma's house, it was in the furniture department. The furniture was sidelined as displays of toys, books, games and play equipment was laid out to attract the attention of children. Trying to choose your Christmas gift was very difficult in the face of so much choice. The other departments also had special Christmas gifts and their windows were full of seasonal gifts, most of which would be bought with the help of the interest-free Doggarts Club.

Wheatley Hill store also had a display of Christmas gifts. By the early 1960s, the store had an extension built that linked the Thornley Road premises to the new building on Wordsworth Avenue, and the two buildings were linked by what I can only describe as a wide tunnel. It was in this tunnel at Christmas that long tables were laid out containing fragrance gifts. It was a sure sign that Christmas was just around the corner when this table appeared in the store.

By the 1960s Christmas trees had lights and ours was always in the bay window of our house in Lynn Terrace. This was our front room, our sitting room, which was decorated with streamers across the ceiling. The back room (our living room) was also decorated with streamers and other decorations but not a Christmas tree.

The making of the Christmas cake was a memorable occasion during my childhood. It was usually baked in October and I can remember my mam buying the currants, sultanas and raisins, washing and drying them and cutting glacé cherries in half, then adding chopped nuts. We didn't have a food mixer in those days and all the ingredients were placed in a big bowl and mixed by hand with a wooden spoon before generous amounts of brandy were added from a half bottle bought for the occasion. Our Christmas cake was always cooked in an electric oven, but my grandma insisted on cooking hers in the coal oven, even though she had an electric one as well. The cake was transferred from the mixing bowl into a cake tin lined with greaseproof paper and brown paper tied around the outside of the tin. My mam always had a smaller tin standing by into which she put a small amount of the Christmas cake mix and called it the trier. The smell in the house while these cakes were cooking was lovely, and a strong indicator that Christmas was on its way. Eventually, after about six hours, the cakes would be lifted out and prodded with a skewer or something similar to see if they were cooked, and left to cool.

We ate the trier over the next few weeks and the main Christmas cake would be stored in an air-tight tin with a quartered apple to keep it moist. The apple was replaced every couple of weeks before the cake was ready for its layer of marzipan, which was secured to the cake with jam. Royal icing was applied to the cake on top of the marzipan and then fluffed up to resemble snow (or so my mam said). She would then wrap a decorative band around the cake and keep it in place with a pin and I put ornaments on the top – we had a Christmas tree, a Santa, a snowman and a sign that said 'Merry Christmas'. These were part of our Christmas cakes for as long as I can remember and by my teenage years quite battered but never replaced. We always opened our Christmas cake at Christmas, but some people didn't open theirs until the New Year, including my grandma.

Both my mam and my grandma had gifts of money set aside for regular tradesmen to their homes and these were known as 'Christmas boxes'. It wasn't a lot of money, but it was tradition in the colliery villages to show these tradesmen how much you appreciated their good service throughout the year. The newspaper delivery boy, the milkman, the binmen and the co-op delivery drivers were all presented with their Christmas boxes on their last visit before Christmas and I remember it took some organising so that they all received their gifts before the big day. After Christmas the same people received a 'glass' (of spirit) and a piece of Christmas cake, in further recognition of their good service.

Also, in the weeks leading up to the big day, my grandma would book in for her Christmas perm at Peggy Carr's (her maiden name and no relation to us), who was married to newsagent Ralph Bell and operated a hairdressing shop at the rear of their newsagent's shop in Alexandra Terrace. This was one of two perms she had during the year, the other being just after Easter and that would see her through the summer holiday period until Christmas.

Santa Claus was talked about and referred to as 'Santy'. We usually spent Christmas Eve with my grandma and granda at Office Street, and after supper my granda made a big thing about wondering whether 'HE' had been. My granda would go up the stairs and come down with a bolster pillowcase filled with presents, wrapped and labelled, and say, 'Aye, he's been', and I would distribute the gifts. They would then be packed up to take home to open on Christmas morning. Walking home to Lynn Terrace on Christmas Eve was special. The pit was quiet, it was usually a frosty and therefore starry night and sometimes it was snowing as we walked down the black path past the allotments to cross the footbridge over the beck to Lynn Terrace.

The next day when I got up, it was to find that Santy had found his way to Lynn Terrace too as I opened presents on Christmas morning. We had our Christmas dinner at home. We never had a turkey for Christmas dinner, we always had a joint of pork together with homemade sage and onion stuffing and Yorkshire puddings. The Christmas vegetables were usually potatoes, Brussels sprouts, carrots and mashed turnip. I can never remember having parsnips. My grandma always had steepy peas on her Christmas dinner, but we didn't. We had a Christmas pudding, but it was never ceremoniously carried into the room wreathed in flames. It was cooked and cut up in the kitchen and brought to the table in portions and served with brandy sauce made with the spare brandy that went in the Christmas cake.

At 3 p.m. everything stopped so that we could watch the Queen's speech on the TV.

On Christmas afternoon, we all travelled to Ludworth to my grandma's sister's house where we had tea and supper and exchanged gifts. My granda and uncle Jack escaped to the Queen's Head public house but my dad, uncle Alf and their cousin Norman, the only other men there and non-drinkers, stayed and joined in with the card games, conversation or TV watching. At some time on Christmas day, my grandma would say, 'Well, all the toys will be broken now.' This became an anticipated statement throughout the rest of her life, and one that made me smile when I became an adult. It is still remembered by my children and remarked upon by them every Christmas Day.

On Boxing Day, my mam was the hostess for teatime, when we would be joined by my grandma and granda and uncle Alf and his family. The occasion followed closely that which we had experienced on Christmas Day and always ended in discussions about a suitable date that we could visit Hebburn to replicate the Christmas hospitality once again, even though it might be February before we got there.

On New Year's Day it was the turn of my grandma to host her seasonal contribution. Hannah and her family from Ludworth were invited for tea and supper, which usually meant catering for a party of about twenty people. We had tea in the dining room at Office Street with the table extended and an assortment of chairs brought from all over the house. The tea was the same every year – cooked ham and pease pudding, hard-boiled egg, tomato, pickled beetroot, pickled onions and mustard in a small pot with its own spoon all served with bread and butter and washed down with cups of tea. There would be home-made sweet mince tarts with white icing on the top instead of pastry, fresh cream cakes and home-made sausage rolls on the table and the meal would be finished with jelly and custard.

It was at these Christmas occasions while helping with the washing up that I was taught how to dry the plates effectively. Pick up two plates, dry the top of one and the bottom of the other and then swap them over, repeating the drying process. A very useful skill to have and one that I could transfer to other washing up situations throughout my life. After the washing up was complete and the crockery stacked away in its cupboard, everyone would congregate in the front sitting room on the back of the house. It had an enormous fireplace and extra seating was brought in to accommodate the guests. The foil milk top decorations were hanging up and their familiar swishing sound could be heard when a door opened, and that was part of our Christmas. My grandma always had a big bowl of peanuts and raisins and a box of dates to pass around. She also had a small New Year's gift for everyone. Some of the adults played cards and some sat around and chatted, but the television was never switched on during these family gatherings. I suppose my grandma felt that a good time could be achieved without it. At some point during the evening the Christmas cake would be cut and distributed with a glass of spirit, usually sherry or whisky, so that everyone could toast the New Year.

My grandma in particular loved Christmas Day at her sister's at Ludworth and New Year's Day in her own home, as a result of the number of her family under one roof. Every member of her close family was important to her and she always valued time spent together, and this extended to new people who became partners of the younger generation.

My grandma and granda didn't celebrate New Year's Eve, except my granda would say every year, 'If you go out now, you'll see a man with as many noses on his face as days left in the year.' This was a bit confusing when I was young, but eventually I realised what he meant, and it was another part of family routine that became special while growing up, and unforgettable overall.

In Lynn Terrace New Year's Eve was a much-looked-forward-to event. Several houses would get together to visit one another after the first foot. In preparation for the new year my mam would take the ashes out of the fire and clean the hearth and make sure the hearth rug had been beaten during the day. The fruit bowl was filled with fruit and the furniture polished. My mam used to justify these preparations by saying that if you were well stocked and clean and tidy on New Year's Eve, then you would remain so throughout the year.

My dad was always our first foot, and he went outside at about 11.55 with his piece of coal and would knock on the door when the pit buzzer sounded at twelve o'clock. He sometimes wasn't ready to come in when my mam answered the door, as he would be exchanging greetings of the season with another first foot neighbour. As I got older, I was allowed to go with my parents to visit the neighbours after twelve o'clock on New Year's morning. I can still remember the feeling of friendliness amongst the gathering as they welcomed us into their homes. Alcohol was readily available at every house, together with some sort of food offering, preparations for this event being planned for in advance, and it was sometimes 4 a.m. when my parents got home to settle down for the night after wishing the neighbours Happy New Year.

The tradition of giving your friends and neighbours a 'glass' (of spirit) and a piece of Christmas cake after Christmas extended well into January as visitors were invited to wish you Happy New Year. My Wingate grandma made very strong ginger wine for this purpose, and I remember visitors to her house being greeted with the wine and a piece of her Christmas cake.

10

EDUCATION

My future would be shaped by the demands of the 1944 Education Act, which was to prepare me for a future as one of the last women of the Durham coalfield. This act raised the school leaving age to 15, so that girls had an extra year in which to gain some leaving qualifications that would better equip them for a successful working life. It introduced the 11-plus examination and made it compulsory for all primary and secondary age pupils to start each school day taking part in collective worship.

By the time I started school at Wheatley Hill Infants Department after Easter 1958, on Monday, 16 April, the education system that was preparing me for my future role in life was already struggling to cope with the demand of the high numbers of post-war children. Having an August birthday was such a disadvantage to a child at that time. Children born between 2 September 1952 and 31 December 1952 started their education in September 1957. Those with birthdays between 1 January 1953 and 30 April 1953 started in January 1958, and those with birthdays between 1 May and 1 September started their education after Easter 1958, six months after the first intake.

Margaret Carr, first school photograph.

According to the school registers of Wheatley Hill Infants Department for 1957–58, twenty-two children joined in September, twenty-three in January and twenty-seven in April, making a year group of seventy-two children in two classes taught by Miss Moon and Mrs Bentley.

As an only child, brought up with mainly adult stimulation at home and without any pre-school preparation, entering an unfamiliar environment filled with children (most of whom I didn't know) and being introduced to an adult who was a stranger was a very daunting experience. I remember the blue tables and chairs and the big fireplace across one corner of the classroom, and not with affection. Everyone seemed to know one another and the routines of the school, and feeling like an outsider, I didn't like being there at all, so when we were allowed to leave the classroom for the first playtime, I took the opportunity to go home. Unfortunately, I was spotted walking down the back of Church Street by the store butcher, who was well known to me as both my mam and grandma were regular customers of his (one of the disadvantages of life in a close-knit community). He realised what was happening and took me home to my mam, who promptly returned me to school with a stern warning. It took me a long time to get over the separation from my preferred environment of home and the adults in my life, and I didn't settle into school life very well or quickly.

Missing my first playtime meant that I also missed the free milk that was available to us and when I was introduced to it the next day, I didn't like it. School milk was introduced into schools by the government in 1945 as they felt that every child should be given one third of a pint every day to help with their development. I remember thinking that this was another reason why I shouldn't stay at school. I declined the offer of the milk, but Miss Moon assured me it was good for me and stood over me while I slowly forced it down. The milk situation got worse in the winter when it became frozen while standing outside and was then defrosted on the school radiators. If it was at all possible, this made it taste even worse, and it felt like a punishment having to drink it.

I always thought it was unfair of my mam to insist that I stayed at school for a school dinner. I had proved I could get home and back in a very short time, but she remained determined that I would be staying and eating my dinner at school, which cost 1s per day (5p). I paid for the whole week on a Monday morning. The dinners were delivered to the school from the school kitchens in Black Road in Mr Race's van. I knew Mr Race because he stored his vans in the old Temperance Hall at the bottom of Jenny's Bank (Patton Street) where I passed every day on my way to school. He delivered a range of large aluminium food containers that held our dinner and sweet and they were set up on tables in the school hall just before lunchtime by the dinner ladies. Once the bell went for lunchtime, and those who were lucky enough to be going home had left the premises, we could queue up at the table nearest our classroom to be served our dinner and take it into the classroom to eat. The food was basic and the same every week. I didn't find the main courses very appealing. My worst experiences were the liver, wet cabbage and tinned tomatoes served with fish (with the skin on) on a Friday; however I enjoyed most of the desserts except prunes served with custard or semolina served with strawberry jam. There was a range of sponge puddings, jam roly-poly and other puddings always served with custard, and sometimes a jelly flan with bananas and custard, which was a particular favourite of mine.

Transferring into the Junior Department in 1961, I was part of the lovely Miss Taylor's class. The two first year junior classes were held in temporary classrooms called the prefabs, and for the first time I was happy at school. This is when I became aware of ability levels and class sets related to ability, but of course it wasn't as easy as that. Most of the pupils in Miss Taylor's class would have May to end of August 1953 birthdays, like me, as she taught the 'B' class. It was assumed that most children starting school six months after the first intake of their year group would not be ready for an 'A' stream education. I have wondered since if this applied to boys and girls equally; were some male Easter starters given the benefit of the 'A' class? But at the time it didn't mean much to me, I just knew that I was in a place where I was happy, with people I liked. I knew I was learning, making progress and was popular with the teacher.

Primary education in the 1960s continued to concentrate on creating a sense of Britishness. Learning traditional country dances in preparation for the Christmas party, singing traditional English folk songs and learning about the history, geography, flora and fauna of the British Empire were all part of our experiences of learning. Nature study was the nearest our lessons got to science. I was happy to be part of the school choir as the choir practice was often held during lesson times, especially if we were practising for a concert. Songs for the choir and for our music lessons during the early 1960s included 'Soldier Soldier Wont You Marry Me', 'Oh No John', 'Up the Airy Mountain' and the 'Raggle Taggle Gypsies'. Our lessons were teacher-led and lots of information required learning by rote and committing it to memory, such as the times tables. I had a good memory and could recite my times tables. I loved reading and writing and, along with the rest of the class, was encouraged to write neatly. I liked the poetry element of our English lessons and one poem that stands out was 'Old Meg the Gypsy'. I remember being asked to copy out the poem into our exercise books and draw a picture of Old Meg, the usual format for poetry learning in those days, and while writing this in 2023 I realise that I can still recite some of the verses of Old Meg's poem.

This idyllic situation lasted for only two terms as Miss Taylor transferred me and Victor Hall into the 'A' class, and while I am sure she did so with the best of intentions, the main one being to give us our best chance of success in education, it turned out to be a disastrous move for me, and my short-lived happiness at school rapidly disappeared. Nothing I did pleased the teacher in the 'A' class, and I quickly lost my new-found confidence in my own abilities and disliked going to school again. From the teacher's point of view, she may have been annoyed at being asked to take two extra children into her teaching group and took it out on me. I wasn't aware if any of her 'A' class pupils transferred into the 'B' class or not. At 7 years old, I was pleasant, well-mannered and conformed easily and I wouldn't have dreamt of answering back or being rude to a teacher, and I couldn't understand why an adult would be so unpleasant to me for no apparent reason, but she was and I was not happy. I asked my mam to intervene. At first, my parents blamed me for making a fuss, but once it became obvious that I wasn't settling down, my mam did eventually arrange a meeting with the headmaster, Mr Wright. Nothing changed. My time in the new class can't have been that long but it seemed like a lifetime. I didn't discuss this with Victor Hall at the time, but wish I had.

Wheatley Hill Junior School.

My second year in the junior school was in the main bottom school building, and I entered that new school year with trepidation and being very wary of any new teacher. It was the first time I had been taught by a man as Mr Alderson became my teacher. We lined up in the school yard in our class groups and marched up the slope, through the cloak-room and into the school where the classrooms were arranged around the school hall, with its shiny, tiled floor. My not-so-good memories of my early days in the new school building were sitting with the rest of the school on the polished floor in the hall listening to the Pilgrim's Progress on a radio that was kept in a very big cupboard and staying behind after school on a Monday to say prayers and sing a hymn in the school hall.

The things I enjoyed about school at that time were the long snow slides made before school started on the smooth, sloping surface of the bottom school yard in the winter and being fearless in sliding down them. There was an overwhelming feeling of disappointment to find they had melted when we came out for playtime. Memorable school trips were to Flamingo Land in 1963 and Tynemouth in 1964; I can't remember any others, but I know they were looked forward to for weeks and enjoyed by all. Ash Wednesday was also an exciting time if you were a regular churchgoer as you were allowed to go to the All Saints Church service during morning lessons. Another thing I looked forward to once I was in the junior school was the freedom to visit the Tin Shop at lunchtime. The Tin Shop wasn't very far from the school, it was near the Royalty cinema and it sold only confectionery. We were allowed to leave the school premises to buy sweets, sherbet, liquorice sticks, barley sugar sticks etc. I had a threepenny piece (3p) most days and spent it on a variety of 'ket'. I notice when reading over the things that I enjoyed about school in the early 1960s, none of them are related to learning!

Sports days were held at the end of every academic year, and we were placed into four 'houses': red (Windsor), yellow (Kent), green (York) and blue (Gloucester). I was in the yellow house, and we were given the appropriate coloured band to wear across our bodies as we competed in different sporting events such as the egg-and-spoon race, the sack race

Junior school trip to Tynemouth, 1964.

and various running races. I had no idea what the colours represented at the time, and if it was explained to me, then I wasn't listening, but realise now that they were probably named after the royal houses. The house that collected the most number of points throughout the day won a shield that went on display in the school hall. We didn't have a PE kit, but sandshoes were provided, and if you could afford them, you could supply your own.

Mr Alderson was my teacher for two years and at the end of my third year in the junior school I was awarded a book prize for merit during the academic year. It was *The Isle of Dogs* by Rosemary Ann Sisson, and I was amazed that I had made any progress at all but even more surprised that somebody had noticed. Mr Alderson must have had some evidence of improvement, as I was still not enjoying school, however when moving into the top class for the final year of my primary education, I enjoyed it much more than I had in the preceding years.

1963

PRIZE

awarded to

Margaret Carr

for

Merit

Wheatley Hill County

Junior Mixed School

J. L. Wright.

Prize for Merit, 1963.

Mr Thompson was a popular teacher; he taught the 'A' class, of which I continued to be a member. He knew I wasn't an all-rounder with regards to my academic work but never made a big deal out of it. He was impressed with a triangle my dad made me for the home-made musical instrument table early in the first term and from our conversations related to musical instruments and my piano lessons and a bit of interest shown in me by the teacher, I began to enjoy schoolwork once again.

I must have told him at some time that I played cricket at home with my family. What I meant was that we played on the path leading to the garden gate in Office Street using the gate as the wicket and with a bat almost as big as me and probably older than my dad, which was very, very heavy. My grandma and granda, my mam and dad, uncle Alf, aunty Nancy, me and Hilary all took part – so it was hardly test match standard, but Mr Thompson included me in his cricket games during the lunch breaks played on the school yard. I was probably the only girl who took part and I never remember batting or bowling but I do remember that I was a good fielder with particularly good catching and throwing skills. I realise now that my dislike of school came from my distrust of teachers as a result of my awful experience in the first year of my junior education, and Mr Thompson did a great deal to restore my faith in the teaching profession.

School parties were much anticipated and were held in the hall after school, but I also remember one being held in the Welfare Hall. The format was always the same and 'The Grand Old Duke of York' stands out as a good ice breaker, together with 'In and Out the Dusty Bluebells', 'The Farmer's in his Den' and 'Miss Mary's Pocket'. This was in addition to the country dancing that we practised at school in the weeks leading up to Christmas, the Dashing White Sergeant, Strip the Willow, the Barn Dance and St Bernard's Waltz. The parties were usually held straight after school, and I can remember attending school in my party clothes with my party shoes (silver or gold) in my bag. I'm sure we had to take our own plate and cup to the party as I remember my mam putting my name on them.

I had managed to keep my place in the 'A' class and my attitude to learning did improve significantly during my final year in the junior school, but the improvements were too little too late. Children in their final year at primary school would normally be training for the 11-plus examination to be selected for the next stage of education, either grammar school, technical grammar school or secondary school, the tripartite system of education introduced under the 1944 Education Act. However, the last 11-plus examination taken by pupils at Wheatley Hill school was in 1963 as it was strongly recognised as being unfair. When I was due to transfer to secondary education therefore, selection was made by primary school recommendations as to which level of education teachers felt their pupils were most suited. The decision-makers must have felt that this type of selection was a much fairer system, although I would question that now, as it must have been open to favouritism by teachers and at risk from pushy parents.

A review from the Wheatley Hill School Register of 1964, the first year the children would be selected by their teacher to attend a secondary school, shows that the year group contained seventy-two children who were taught in two classes by Mr Thompson in the 'A' class and Miss Hart in the 'B' class. The majority of pupils transferred to either the girls' secondary school in Wordsworth Avenue or the boys' secondary school in the front street. They would be joined by pupils from Thornley Primary School, with a relatively small number transferring to the grammar school and an even smaller number to the technical school at Shotton, where it was still possible to take part in the GCE 'O' level examinations. Pupils attending Shotton School from the natural feeder schools didn't wear a uniform, however those selected to attend from other villages as a result of the 11-plus selection wore a uniform and were taught alongside one another.

I had eventually made steady progress with my education, gaining confidence and pride from my achievement award. My arithmetic had improved and my reading and writing skills were very good, but it was not enough to gain a place at the grammar school. Showing a great insight into the lack of academic and career opportunities available to women at the time, my parents were keen my mam and dad were keen for me to attend a private school in order to enhance my life chances. Both of my parents regretted their lack of achievement in their own education, which was self-inflicted and very much regretted in the case of my dad. My mam felt let down by her Roman Catholic education, which she always described as 'Catechism heavy'. As a result, they were keen for me to have opportunities not available to or taken up by them. As I was an only child, they were prepared to make this investment to ensure that I had access to opportunities consistent with a grammar school education. However, after my mixed experiences of education so far, and how quickly situations in that arena could change and how slowly I adapted to that change, I couldn't think of anything worse than having to attend a school in a town away from my friends. Remembering the horror of my first days, weeks and months when I started school, which seemed to go on forever, and then the disaster in the first year junior class, I wouldn't go along with their plans. This is a decision I didn't regret, but it was a gesture I still consider incredible.

The period after the Second World War was a time of great change, as previously mentioned, and the 1944 Education Act was one of the significant changes. The Act raised the school leaving age to 15, with all students required to stay in full-time education until then, and the change was largely aimed at girls' education. The government felt that if girls stayed in education for longer, they would reach significantly higher levels and be more prepared for work and other educational opportunities.

Wheatley Hill was well equipped for secondary education where vocational subjects were part of the curriculum. The schools were used by children from both Thornley and Wheatley Hill. The boys' department was in the front street (referred to locally as the big boys' school) and the girls' provision, built in 1938, was in Wordsworth Avenue: Wheatley Hill Peter Lee Girls Secondary Modern School (referred to locally as the big girls' school).

Pupils from the mining villages who attended the grammar school had the opportunity to take examinations and progress to higher education but only if they stayed at school for an extra year, until they were 16. The opportunity to improve the life chances of their children was an ambition held by many parents, who also believed that their children should achieve more than they had with the amount of opportunities they were presented with, and there is no doubt that if hard-working children with supportive parents attended the grammar school they could achieve upward social mobility. However, many children attending the grammar school left at 15 without taking full advantage of their education, whereas staying on for an extra year may have provided them with the reward of GCE 'O' level examinations that would have opened doors to junior positions in clerical jobs such as branch banking, the civil service and coal board administration. Attending a secondary modern school in most cases could not improve the life chances of pupils, particularly girls, and it was this disparity that caused debate within the government about the introduction of comprehensive education – a system thought by some to be fairer to all children.

The core curriculum was taught in the girls' secondary modern with the addition of needlework, PE, art and domestic science, aimed at preparing the girls, even in the mid-1960s, for their future domestic role in life, in which a husband and children would be their main priority. Knitting and sewing were not high on my mam's agenda, therefore it was never important to me either. My grandma tried to interest me and taught me to knit but I didn't enjoy it. My lack of needlework skills were highlighted during my first year in the secondary school when we were expected to make our cap and apron in readiness for cookery lessons in the second year. Both of my pieces were a disaster and while some girls had completed their items by Christmas, I had to take mine home in the summer holidays for my grandma to finish off for me. Mrs Standish, the needlework teacher, despaired of my hand stitching and lack of sewing machine skills, and when I took my apron to show her my progress, without speaking or even looking at me, she just handed it back to be unpicked and redone. The seams on the apron in particular were very dirty from excessive unpicking. It is fair to say that the sewing skills on which my female ancestors depended died out with me.

In the short term, girls from the secondary school were guided towards unskilled work aged 15 in retail, factories or auxiliary nursing, all related to 'work' and not 'career'. Boys attending a secondary modern school were in a much stronger position as jobs and apprenticeships were available to them from the National Coal Board, as well as other job providers outside the coal industry such as distribution, retail and building trades, all of which could improve their life chances and include, if they were willing, the opportunity to study at further and even higher education.

At the end of the second year at Wheatley Hill Peter Lee Girls Secondary Modern School, pupils were offered an opportunity to study a commercial course in years three and four or follow the normal school curriculum with more emphasis on domestic science and needlework, preparing girls to serve – either in marriage or in a job where these skills would be recognised.

The commercial course at Wheatley Hill school was set up in 1955 and provided the only vocational training for girls. It included the study of commerce, accounts, typewriting, shorthand and office practice, alongside English Language and English Literature. Lessons in art, needlework and domestic science were not necessary to those following this

Wheatley Hill Peter Lee Girls' Modern School.

course, which offered girls the opportunity of either gaining office skills appropriate for employment as an office junior at age 15 or moving to a technical college to upgrade their skills. All girls in the fourth and final year of secondary school would be entered into the Northern Counties examinations in the school subjects they were following.

In 1968, and for the first time, Wheatley Hill secondary schools offered pupils the opportunity to stay in full-time education for a further year following a Certificate in Secondary Education Course (CSE) that was available in both academic and vocational subjects. This was five years before the official Raising of the School Leaving Age (ROSLA) was introduced nationally and it gave pupils from second-ary modern schools the opportunity to follow a course of study and achieve a qualification at the end of their compulsory education that was recognised by both employers and further education providers.

In 1968 the two secondary schools in Wheatley Hill became co-edu-cational, with boys and girls taught in mixed groups over the two sites, in the front street and in the Wordsworth Avenue premises. The head teacher at the girls' school, Miss Alderslade, retired after forty-three years at the school in July 1968 and the head teacher from the boys' school, Mr Harris, became head teacher of the amalgamated school.

Most working-class parents of children at a secondary modern school, along with their children, were impatient to get their education out of the way and into work, and out of 100 pupils (boys and girls) leaving school at Wheatley Hill in 1968, I was one of only fifteen from the two schools who took advantage of staying on for a fifth year in order to follow the CSE course of study. There were five boys and ten girls in the first fifth year at Wheatley Hill School.

The higher number of girls is significant and it may have meant that parents were becoming more ambitious for their daughters and encouraging them to stay at school longer, recognising that working hard at school to pass exams would improve their life chances. Or it could be that staff in the all-girls school had been persuasive in pointing out how the extra year would help them gain a place at one of the local technical colleges offering a range of business-related courses in secretarial work and also business administration, which most had been following at school. It is also possible that the girls themselves were becoming more aware of what a good education could offer them in the long term. However, the teacher of commercial subjects was inspirational, and I believe that was one of the main factors taken into account when making the decision to stay at school for an extra year or leave.

Some pupils who may have wanted to stay on for an extra year at school may have been discouraged from doing so by their parents. Children were expensive, and if they stayed in education they would need to be supported financially for a further year by families who may have budgeted for their school leavers to earn their own living after 1968.

The extra year at school was psychologically important. We all knew we were the first pupils to have a fifth year at Wheatley Hill schools and gained a certain pride in that. We were referred to by lower year groups, particularly the fourth-year boys, as 'the upper fifth' in a humorous/sarcastic way that seemed to acknowledge the uniqueness of the situation. However, no doubt they may have also felt aggrieved that they should have been at the top of the school and had been prevented from doing so by these fifteen people who stayed on for an extra year.

We were grown up and we could could have been at work, but we had chosen to improve our life chances at school and that brought with it some pride in ourselves. Teachers treated us differently. We enjoyed excellent relationships with them, those from the girls' school that we already knew, and eventually, when they got used to us, the male teachers from the boys' school. Mr Jones took an interest in my guitar playing and gave me and my friend Pauline lunchtime tuition, which improved our skills no end. We were all made prefects and had a badge to show our authority. The staff were more friendly and relied on us for help with a range of tasks, including organising a Christmas variety show in which we were the main performers. Our PE lessons consisted of badminton only, which I was very pleased about. That was another area of my education that I had worked very hard to avoid over the years, but I did enjoy badminton and table tennis. As a result of our maturity, we were allowed to play badminton during our lunchtime too. Being a member of the fifth form was an amazing transformation as developing young people, and I believe we all viewed our education differently during the extra year.

I thrived during my fifth year at Wheatley Hill secondary school. For the first time since my education began, I realised that I had some potential within education as I tackled the higher-level commercial subjects. I loved the daily practice needed to succeed in both shorthand and typewriting, and the rigour and importance of learning the many, many rules surrounding Isaac Pitman's New Era shorthand. I firmly believe that I achieved more in the months from September 1968 to June 1969 than I had in the rest of my education to date. The inspirational Miss Stamp was the teacher delivering the commercial course and the success of all the girls following that course was a testament to her excellent teaching methods. With only nine girls in the group (one was following an art-related curriculum), the quality of teaching, learning and the pace of learning was much more effective and led to an increased self-belief and level of confidence within the girls that was obvious and transferrable into other situations in education and life. The door was now open for further education, higher education, employment or all three, to girls who didn't attend a grammar school and came from working-class backgrounds. This was a door that was either firmly closed or only partially open to my female ancestors.

11

WOMEN IN THE 1960S

My mam was typical of a woman of her generation and status in the 1960s who had no educational qualifications, job-related training, or aspirations for either of those two things. Her employment with Walter Willson's grocery store ended when she married as this was their company policy. It wasn't a priority for many working-class women to take up full-time employment and they were happy to engage in part-time work that would fit in with their care-giving duties at home, their main aim being to add to the family budget and not to develop a career. The jobs that these women became involved in were mostly unskilled, part-time, low paid and easy to access from their homes, and my mam began such a part-time job once I started school.

The Marriage Bar that had restricted the employment of married women from the late nineteenth century was still in place in the 1960s and although not a legal requirement, it was still operated by some employers. It became an expectation of some employers that once a woman married, she would leave her paid employment and become a housewife, making her husband and family her priority. It is fair to say that it was also an expectation of some women that they would only work until they married, and some women believed it was selfish for a woman to continue working after marriage as she was withholding a position that could be offered to a single woman.

After the significant contribution women had made to the workplace during the Second World War, the Marriage Bar was relaxed, and married women in teaching or who worked in a bank or the civil service could continue working after their marriage. It still, however, existed in many jobs. Apart from having to leave a job upon marriage, the Marriage Bar also disqualified married women from applying for some vacancies. The employment of women was described by one government department in the early 1950s as 'a perfect nuisance', referring of course to the likelihood of her having a family and leaving her job.

Female workers for the Co-operative Wholesale Society in the 1960s were required to resign from their job when they married. The Society was a significant employer of both male and female school leavers in the colliery villages, and having a job in the 'store' was considered to be a 'step up'. However, when women announced their plans to marry, they were forced to leave even in the late 1960s, while their male colleagues who had joined the organisation at the same time were on to the first stages in their management training. Women carrying out similar jobs to men in any job would expect to be paid much less, and even if a newly married woman wanted to make a career within the Co-op, it wasn't possible and the best she could expect was to apply for a part-time post.

There weren't any rules regarding the Marriage Bar, and it was interpreted differently from employer to employer. It wasn't until 1975 and the introduction of the Sex Discrimination Act that the practice stopped altogether.

My mam became an agent for Doggarts department store at Wingate in 1959. My dad was bringing home £9 a week from his job as a mechanical fitter at Wheatley Hill pit, and the Doggarts pay, while small, would be welcome.

Doggarts had seventeen shops throughout County Durham. The owner of the chain, Mr Doggart, set up the Doggarts Club, an interest-free way for families to buy a range of goods from the store by buying a Club for different amounts and repaying it weekly without the addition of interest. My mam was one of 800 collecting staff travelling across County Durham collecting payments from Doggarts customers. This method of purchasing goods was essential for low-paid workers, who could spread the cost of their expenditure without the need to save up, which was often impossible on low wages. My mam's area was the lower end of Wheatley Hill and on a Friday she visited customers who had taken out a Club in order to collect the payments that would reduce their overall balance. During the school holidays I would go with her on these visits and then travel by bus to North Road, Wingate, where she dropped off the payments she had collected with Mr Ball, a representative of the store. As a result of my mam working for Doggarts, most of our spending was carried out there and not at the co-operative store like my Wheatley Hill grandma. Doggarts had pneumatic change dispensers that travelled across the ceilings of the Wingate shop to a central point, returning your change to the department you were in. I also remember the distinctive green bags with gold writing that Doggarts was famous for.

Factory work and shop work were available during the 1960s for girls leaving school without qualifications and for those who wanted a job in their home village. The pyjama factory in the old Embassy Ballroom and the anorak factory in the Wesleyan Chapel that had closed some years before offered this opportunity in Wheatley Hill. This sort of employment gave married women the chance to contribute to the family budget and single women the possibility of earning a living, particularly if they had existing sewing skills. The advantages of working at these two outlets was that it was local, therefore there was no need to travel, and the work unskilled, although training was given in sewing machine skills that would become transferable to similar situations.

There were other employment opportunities for women without qualifications from Wheatley Hill and the surrounding colliery villages. Roles related to having a job and not a career could be found at Paton & Baldwins knitting factory in Darlington and Smart & Browns electronics in Spennymoor. These both provided transport to and from work, and in 1960 the Tudor crisp factory at Peterlee became another major employer of female labour that offered the advantage of shift work so that women could fit in their work commitments around their care-giving. Tudor Foods also offered transport one way, either early morning or late evening, when public transport was not available.

There were more opportunities available for a girl who had gained qualifications at the grammar school, even if she left school at 15 with GCE 'O' levels, or a girl who had attended one of the secretarial colleges to gain office-related qualifications. Clerical jobs were available in a range of places. From the National Coal Board head office at Castle Eden or Spennymoor, to individual colliery offices, to branch banking throughout local towns and council offices at Easington or Durham. Two Wheatley Hill girls even found employment at Greatham airport, having left secretarial college in 1956.

My grandma's sister Hannah and her family at Ludworth bought the Ludworth shop and Post Office from Douglas Hall at the end of the 1950s and her daughter Rene was installed as the post mistress, with both Hannah and daughter Mavis helping out in the shop.

Hannah Grainger in Ludworth Shop and Post Office.

It was my favourite family outing to visit Ludworth. Visits were usually when the shop was closed but my grandma supported the business by buying grocery items and I, supervised by one of the adults, was allowed to serve her. I was taught how to write down the items she was buying and add them up and how to give her change. This was a very useful learning experience for me, and one that I was successful at, and helped towards building my confidence and subsequent improvement in arithmetic tasks.

The sharp increase in marriages in the early 1940s can be attributed to the Second World War and the need felt by many to formalise their relationship, particularly if the man was in the armed forces. There was always the possibility of the man being killed and by marrying he could allocate part of his pay to his wife. If he was killed in action, she would receive a pension. However, there was a large increase in the number of divorces towards the end of the 1940s, as many found that they weren't as compatible as they thought they would be. As a result, divorce rates reached an all-time high by 1946. While divorce among the working classes was still rare at this time, both Rene and Mavis, who married during the 1940s, were divorced by the early 1960s, each with a child. They now lived with their parents once again in the Post Office on North View, the purchase of which was probably as a result of the need for employment by both women and so that care-giving could be shared among the family. Divorce was seen as a regrettable necessity by the working classes, but they tended to agree that if a marriage was unhappy and differences couldn't be resolved then it was sometimes the only answer. However, there was still a stigma attached to it, especially in small communities.

Rene and Mavis had so much in common with their great grandmother, Hannah. They had, like her, gone against what society expected of them, separating from their husbands. Like her, they saw self-employment as an alternative to going out to work after the break-up of their relationships. In Hannah's case, it was perhaps her only option as paid employment for women of her age was rare in Ludworth. In both cases, seventy years apart, Hannah and her great-granddaughters turned to retail, trading from home in Ludworth.

Unlike their great grandmother, Rene and Mavis didn't remarry quickly. Marrying for a second time in Hannah's day was a popular thing to do. It gave a woman who had been widowed some financial security and it gave a widower help in the home including, perhaps, childcare. We'll never know why, but Hannah took the unusual step of leaving her second husband and setting up a shop on her own in private rented accommodation, taking in lodgers in order to help her pay the rent. It was a very high-risk approach at the time, but one that paid off, and it showed a determination and strength of character that both her great-granddaughters demonstrated seventy years later. Their situation, in being able to pool resources with their parents and unmarried brother Norman, was a lot less risky but led to them both gaining employment from the venture, both women following in the entrepreneurial footsteps of their great-grandmother in the same street of the same village!

With the need to earn a living, the two women involved themselves in other businesses too. Mavis ran two market stalls in Durham indoor market on a Saturday and collectively they bought property in Durham City to rent out as student accommodation. This was another good example of a family pulling together when one (or two) of them falls on hard times. By all living under the same roof in the Post Office, they each had the help and support that intergenerational living provided.

With the security of a good marriage, my mam proved over the next few years that she was a very good businesswoman as she took on two projects suggested by my dad's cousin and now businesswoman, Mavis. My mam was always confident and outgoing and, as it turned out, also ambitious and determined, the opposite of my dad's personality. He was much less confident and reserved but quietly ambitious, perhaps not for himself but for my mam and me. My mam was particularly interested in the buy-to-rent property business that Mavis had made such a success of on behalf of her family, and felt it was a good opportunity for future investment for our family. However, with so little money by way of savings available to them apart from my dad's pay from the pit and my mam's part-time wages from Doggarts, my dad was rightly cautious. After long discussions with his cousin and the

Durham Indoor Market.

obvious commitment and enthusiasm of my mam, whom he trusted as a sound and skilful financial manager and hard worker, they assessed the situation and decided that the risk was minimal if they were sensible. They took on another mortgage and bought a three-storey property on The Avenue, Durham City, the need for student accommodation in the town ensuring that the mortgage payments were covered by the rents they received.

In 1966 the second business opportunity presented itself, once again provided by Mavis, when my parents bought her two stalls in Durham indoor market that sold confectionery. As she had a background in the retail trade before her marriage, this opportunity appealed to my mam and after looking at the accounts to project the likely takings in the future, she continued to run the two stalls and slowly increased the product range as she and my dad visited different wholesalers and increased their turnover. I was 13 by this time and the sweet stalls on the market provided me with Saturday employment throughout my early teenage years.

There is no doubt that my mam was the driving force behind both ventures. The business was significantly E. & G. Carr, which appeared on the stalls and on business stationery and confirmed her lead. My dad was a naturally cautious person, but he trusted my mam's business acumen and supported her and the two businesses.

12

GROWING UP
IN THE 1960S

Looking back on growing up in a mining village you become aware of the social cohesion, social networks and strict division of gender roles that existed. For generations colliery villages, because of their isolated locations, had provided their own entertainments. There had always been outlets for men's entertainment such as the working men's and social clubs, chapel and church groups and sporting teams, but after the Second World War women's groups grew in number as they started to build their own social networks and the Women's' Institute, Mothers' Club and female-only groups associated with the church and chapel became more popular. My mam was a member of the WI, which met in the Miners' Welfare Hall on a Tuesday night and as a child I always thought it was odd that on WI nights she went out with a cup, saucer and plate in her bag.

Even in the 1960s when road and transport links were good, there were still plenty of opportunities for entertainment within the village for children and young people. There was a very active group of cubs, brownies, scouts and guides, dancing classes, youth clubs at the Miners' Welfare Hall and at the church and chapel, afternoon matinees at both cinemas, and the Girls Friendly Society at the church as well as the opportunity to join the church choir. Children also made their own entertainment. Bike ownership was popular and there was a variety of play equipment in the recreation ground in the Miners' Welfare Park. The pit heaps, quarries and Bonsie's pond (Burn's Brickyard Pond) also provided unofficial outdoor play areas for the children of Wheatley Hill. We all had sledges, most made at the pit, and there were lots of places to slide down, the most dangerous being Jenny's Bank (Patton Street was named Jenny's Bank as Jenny's shop was situated there). The bank was a main road with an unguarded colliery railway line running across the bottom and while I cannot recall any accidents, I do recall being told not to use my sledge there, but it was a long, steep hill and provided the best slide. Perhaps a more dangerous sledge run was beside the steps leading from Gowland Terrace up to the pit workshops. It was much steeper, shorter and therefore faster than Patton Street as you slid across the main vehicle access road leading to Lynn Terrace. I was warned against that run too.

Games of cricket that went on for hours were played on the 'new' road leading to Lynn Terrace. We had to move the wickets every time a car came up or down the road, but that wasn't very often. Roller skating was popular throughout my childhood, and the space outside of the pit baths provided a great skating surface but it was only available when the pit was quiet, on a weekend. We played two-bally with the well-known rhymes passed on such as: 'Mrs toffee apple ball, went to see a waterfall, she fell in and couldn't swim, Mrs toffee apple ball', the balls hitting the wall in time with the rhyme. Skipping with elastic bands tied together around our ankles was another popular game, as were chucks and marbles. We fished in the beck with a colourful net bought from Jenny's shop, keeping the fish in a jam jar and returning them to the beck when we finished fishing. We caught bees on the big purple weeds growing on the slum clearance land of the old colliery streets, saving them in jam jars too and releasing them when we tired of the pastime, or were stung. The days of a child in the 1960s were spent outside and parents never expected to see their children from early morning until they went home to eat, and they knew they didn't need to worry.

There was one incident, however, that involved many of the children from Lynn Terrace and caused our parents to worry when we took tomatoes from Mr Wilson's greenhouse. Mr Wilson from No. 4, like my granda, was recognised as a very good gardener and had two greenhouses in which he grew lots of tomatoes. I don't know who the ringleaders were, but I was only about 5 years old, and the older girls showed me how to make my dress into a holder for tomatoes by lifting the hem up. I didn't pick any tomatoes, I just had to make my dress available to carry them, and I have no idea what we were going to do with them. I just know that as I struggled home with my haul of tomatoes, my parents, along with all other parents of children involved in the incident, were angry as they returned the mountain of tomatoes to the even angrier Mr Wilson.

There were lots of children of all ages in Lynn Terrace and we all worked together collecting for the bonfire, a firm item on the calendar as all areas in the village prepared for 5 November. The bonfire at Lynn Terrace was held on the grassed area in front of the houses near the road bridge, and collecting items to burn began in September. The nearest rival bonfire was at the top of Patton Street and one of the exciting challenges was to keep our bonfire collection safe from Llewy Jones from the Patton Street bonfire. It was always rumoured that his gang would come and raid our bonfire and we went to great lengths to protect it. However, I don't ever remember such an attack, but it did add to the excitement. Mr Lamb from No. 13 seemed to take control of lighting the bonfire on 5 November as we all stood around and watched the efforts of our labours go up in smoke together with our guy dressed immaculately in anything we could find. Once the fire burned down, we threw our potatoes into the embers to cook and happily ate the often burnt offering that the potato became.

I started piano lessons when I was 8 years old with my earliest friend Robert Facey from Lynn Terrace. We were about the same age and his mam and my mam had been friends since we were born. The Faceys had a piano and we didn't, so Mrs Facey gave me the opportunity to learn alongside Robert. Mr Williams came from Ludworth on a Monday evening at about 5 p.m. and the lessons cost 3s 6d (17p). Robert had the first lesson and then it was my turn. Learning to play any musical instrument needs daily practice, and Mrs Facey didn't mind me going to their house almost every day for half an hour. Eventually my parents bought me a good second-hand piano and I can imagine Mrs Facey being delighted, not having to listen to two lots of intermittent pianists on a daily basis!

Being an only child, there was no expectation of me to help with chores around the house. I enjoyed helping my grandma to bake or pick flowers, fruit and vegetables from the garden, and I would often be sent to Jenny's shop in Patton Street to collect items forgotten from the store order. On a Saturday morning after we had been to the lamp cabin I would often go with my granda to the front street, where he would pay the newspaper bill at Hodgson's, on one occasion telling my grandma when we got back, 'Ye'd think she'd led a blind man about, she knew everybody we've met this morning.' My granda had a lot of these little sayings and while I didn't fully understand what he meant at the time, they both found it very funny.

I was an avid reader from an early age and a member of Wheatley Hill library. Eventually I had read all of the Enid Blyton books in the library and moved on to more sophisticated reading. As well as my library books, I also became a convert to the weekly comic papers in the early 1960s. My first magazine was *June*, which was delivered weekly from Hodgson's paper shop and paid for on my mam's newspaper bill. I read it from cover to cover and collected the *June* annuals every Christmas. However, by 1965 I had outgrown *June*, and anyway she had amalgamated with *School Friend* and wasn't the same, and I moved on to *Jackie*. *Jackie* was much more sophisticated for 12-year-olds. It had a problem page – 'Dear Cathy & Claire' – fashion and beauty tips, gossip, short stories, competitions and comic strips, and the centre pages were usually a pull-out poster of a band or film star. It was essential reading for developing females, who even in the 1960s would not be given any relationship advice either at home or at school. Most of my friends read *Jackie* and it was a popular talking point as we tiptoed our way through the issues associated with developing into adults.

I was there when the first programme of *Coronation Street* was broadcast in December 1960 and I looked forward to the Sunday afternoon TV drama adaptation from children's literature such as *Jane Eyre*, *Great Expectations* and *Oliver Twist*, among others. Sundays were a day for church and Sunday lunch but after that it was such a dull day. I don't remember even visiting my grandma and granda on a Sunday in the winter.

When *Top of the Pops* started in 1964, I tuned in on a Thursday night when I could, keeping up to date with 1960s pop music, and then when Radio 1 began in September 1967 and Tony Blackburn became a household name, I asked for a transistor radio for Christmas so that I could listen regularly. Once I had my own radio, I listened religiously to *Pick of the Pops* on a Sunday evening presented by Alan Freeman. We had a Grundig reel-to-reel tape recorder that my dad bought from Mervyn Hodgson's at Wingate in the late 1950s and I started to record the *Pick of the Pops* songs I liked so that I could play them through the week. My parents wouldn't hear of buying a record player.

Despite having had a television set since 1953, my grandma and granda never switched it on before the news at 6 p.m. and then it became their entertainment for the rest of the evening if they weren't planning on going out anywhere. On a Saturday evening in the winter, we would all sit around the TV in Office Street and watch *Dixon of Dock Green* and *The Billy Cotton Band Show*.

My Wingate grandma and granda didn't have a TV set. They couldn't afford one and if they saw a programme advertised in the newspaper that they would like to see they went to the working men's club to watch it. My granda was a fan of *The Black and White Minstrel Show*. He always maintained that a man from Wingate was a regular performer in the show, Maurice Sodey, but I was never sure that was true. Probably as a result of not having a TV, both my grandma and granda were prolific readers and visited Wingate library regularly, at least two and sometimes three times a week.

My growing up in the 1960s included my first direct experience of death when my Wingate granda, Jim Unsworth, died. He was 66 years old. I wasn't as close to my Wingate grandparents as I was to my Wheatley Hill ones, but I loved them and can remember when I was younger worrying about what would happen when my grandparents died. I was 13 at the time of his death and his passing hit me hard. The adults may have been expecting it, but they didn't tell me, and I wasn't. As with all instances of sudden change in my life up to then, I didn't deal with it very well.

My granda was an avid reader as I was, and he always showed an interest in the books I was reading. He used to take me for a walk to the welfare park in Wingate and we would watch the bowling, chatting all the time about this and that. He would tell me about his time in the Army during the Second World War and unfortunately I didn't listen too closely to his stories except for one. When he was stationed in Ireland he was allocated an Alsatian dog for his sentry duty. One night when they were on patrol, it came on to rain very heavily and the dog went into the sentry box and wouldn't let my granda in and he got soaking wet during the rest of his duty. I thought this was very funny as a child, and I think looking back on it so did he.

My mam's oldest sister, my aunty Alice, came from Cumberland for the funeral but I wasn't allowed to go. I canvassed each one of the adults separately, but the answer was the same, 'a funeral is no place for a child'. I was sent off to school as if nothing had happened because the adults said it was for the best, and I remember having a particularly bad day at school on the day of the funeral. He was buried at the Roman Catholic St Peter's and Paul's Church, Hutton Henry, in a grave without a headstone.

My Wheatley Hill granda had owned a car since 1945 and upgraded it twice by the 1960s but he didn't like to drive, so my dad did the driving. In the summer months on a Saturday and Sunday evening we would go for a drive to locations around the area. Some of the places had a significance to me as a child of under 10 years old: Seaton Carew – amusement arcades; Crimdon – paddling pool in the dene; Seaburn – the Guinness Clock and shuggy boats; Redcar – helter-skelter and shuggy boats. However, there were a large number that didn't as we seemed to visit an endless number of garden-related attractions that all looked the same to me.

We also had events throughout the year that we visited – Appleby Fair, various race meetings, Yarm Fair, Durham Miners Gala, several air shows and Durham Regatta, and the five us also went on an annual holiday to different locations in England, Scotland or Wales. It was always the pit fortnight and my grandma kept up the holiday diary started by my granda in the 1940s that listed where we went, where we stayed, what we saw and an evaluation at the end of the holiday as to how much she had enjoyed it.

One of my most memorable childhood holidays was in 1958 when we planned a trip to Wales to visit my grandma's nephew, Douglas, the son of her sister, Rachel, who died a few days after he was born in 1918. Douglas was brought up by my great grandma, Susan, helped by

Douglas Williamson, RAMC.

my grandma and her sister, Hannah. He lived with my grandma and granda at Thornley when they first married and had always been very close to the family.

During the Second World War Douglas signed up and enlisted in the Royal Army Medical Corps and was posted to the Mid Wales Hospital, Talgarth, in the Brecon Beacons, when the hospital was taken over by the Army in 1940. He remained at the hospital as a male nurse after the war ended when it returned to its psychiatric status, and met and married fellow nurse Carol Hopkins in 1946.

My grandma kept in touch with Douglas by letters and Christmas cards but hadn't met Carol or their daughter Marion, so, in 1958, Wales was the destination for our annual holiday to spend one week with Douglas, Carol and Marion. As was usual with all our holidays, it was documented in my grandparents' holiday diary, which states that we set off from Wheatley Hill in my granda's Wolseley 4/44 at 8.15 a.m. on Saturday, 5 July 1958. We had lunch at Preston, Lancashire, and tea at Church Stretton, Shropshire, arriving at Talgarth at 8 p.m.

1958 Holiday to Wales with Mr and Mrs Todd
from Wheatley Hill (on the right).

The weather during the week in Wales was lovely and sunny as we travelled around the Welsh countryside with Douglas and his family, each trip being carefully recorded and added to the holiday diary. We visited Barry Island, Merthyr Tydfil, Pontypridd, Cardiff, Tenby and New Quay, where coincidentally we met Mr and Mrs Todd from Gowland Terrace, Wheatley Hill, also holidaying in Wales.

It was a lovely holiday and, with improvements in private transport and better road systems over the years, led to a close relationship with our Welsh family, who we saw perhaps once a year as they travelled to Durham or we travelled to Wales. On occasions we also met up to holiday in Scotland.

Socialisation of early teenagers in the colliery villages happened within the village. In my time growing up there, when I was ready to go 'out', it had to be something that was acceptable to my parents, and given the isolated location of Lynn Terrace, only if someone else from

Wheatley Hill Church Hall.

141

the street was going. My 'going out' started by going to the Royalty with friends from school on a Friday evening and by gaining my parents' trust and coming in at the time they stipulated, gradually I was able to go further afield (still in Wheatley Hill). When I was 14, I joined the All Saints Church youth club, which was held in the church hall on a Sunday evening after Evensong. I was a Sunday School teacher by this time and the youth club on a Sunday evening appealed to me. The rule was that if you attended Evensong then you could go to the youth club, but eventually we found ways around this rule. It was run by older church-going teenagers and was a fantastic environment in which to 'grow up'.

I had taught myself to play the guitar by this time and was encouraged to play and sing at the youth club. Eventually five us got together to form a folk group and we held folk nights in the church hall and often entertained at church social and other events. The youth club committee obtained permission from the church council to turn one of

All Saints Folk Group, L–R: Jean Oliver, Tommy Hodgson, Margaret Carr, Pauline Nicholson. Front: Robert Waite, Derek Ayre (manager).

the small rooms in the church hall into a coffee bar and we all helped clean, paint and decorate the room. The boys who were following joinery apprenticeships made a coffee bar, and with its coloured lighting and posters it was an excellent example of a folk club in the mid-1960s. It seems, because we were all involved in creating this space, that we all took collective responsibility for looking after it. We did our own clearing up and didn't expect anyone else to do it for us. We organised our own stock control and made sure our products were relevant to the needs of our customers.

We planned regular youth club trips to the newly opened Billingham Forum, a sports and leisure complex containing a swimming pool, ice rink, a number of sporting facilities and a theatre. Ice skating was my thing but once in Billingham there was also a ten-pin bowling alley very near the Forum and as long as we were back at the bus at the allocated time for leaving, no one minded where we went. We usually booked Nicholson's bus and were responsible for collecting payment for the bus fares and paying the money to Mr Nicholson.

We obtained permission from the church council to lay out a badminton court on the church hall floor and began to play badminton there on a Friday evening, while some of the joinery boys made two table tennis tables with materials donated by local timber merchant Tony Carr. The badminton sessions became so popular and attracted so many people that we had to change our venue to the Miners' Welfare Hall, where we could service two badminton courts at the same time and ran that club on two nights a week.

While the benefit of working together with a group was probably overlooked as being unimportant at the time, I can see now how vital the above activities were in creating an atmosphere where, as a young person, you could take risks, make mistakes, offer suggestions, be listened to and become involved in a range of activities, including an introduction to the formal structures needed for committees etc., all in a safe environment. Looking back, I still feel privileged to have been part of the youth club as I believe it contributed massively to my personal development.

The Miners' Welfare committee continued to play a major role in providing recreational activities through the Miners' Welfare Park and Hall in Wheatley Hill and the annual colliery village sports day. It was an event that was looked forward to by all. Organised by the committee, the afternoon started with a parade of our colliery band and in 1967 five jazz bands from Thornley, Horden, Peterlee, Felling and Burnmoor took part in the procession, marching from the colliery offices through the village to the big girls' school field in Wordsworth Avenue.

Adults and children joined in the fancy dress parade and they were judged on the school field and prizes awarded for the winners. Almost all households supported the sports day and lined the streets to watch the parade and bands, many following them to the sports field to watch the judging of competitions and prize-giving.

In 1967 the judges of the fancy dress were the colliery manager and his wife, Mr and Mrs Richardson, the under-manager and his wife, Mr and Mrs Bowman, the Rev. and Mrs Henderson from the Methodist church and Mrs G.G. Graham, wife of the vicar of All Saints. Every child who took part in the fancy dress parade received a 2s (10p) savings stamp and 1,800 children up to school-leaving age whose fathers worked at the pit received a bag of sweets to the value of 3s 6d (17p). The event also included field events for children and a 4-mile race from the school field, along the A181 towards Wingate, down the slack bank to Thornley Crossings and then back to Wheatley Hill past the pit and the front street to the school field. The winner of this event was also presented with a prize.

Wheatley Hill Scouts helped to provide sideshows and women's organisations provided tea and refreshments. Prizes for a lucky draw were provided by the working men's club and the Soldiers and Sailors Club. It was an excellent example of a small community all pulling together to make sure everyone had a good time, and the local newspaper reported that 5,000 people attended the sports day that year.

13

ENFORCED CHANGES

Since nationalisation in 1947 there had been substantial changes in the working conditions in Britain's coal mines that included more supervision down the pit. A guaranteed weekly wage was introduced together with a five-day week and two weeks' paid holidays. Pithead baths and canteens became the norm instead of the exception, and were appearing at most collieries. A national safety scheme was introduced, as well as a training scheme for all new starters at the pit. In addition, boys were not allowed to go down into the pit until they were 16 years of age. Investment in modern machinery led to greatly increased productivity as miners became among the highest-paid manual workers, and at the end of the 1940s coal was in high demand. With no significant rival, the future looked good.

The new equipment brought its own problems, and the amount of dust it generated was one of the main complaints made by coal miners. This necessitated the introduction of water sprays underground to cut down on the amount of coal dust in the air. Sprays were installed at Wheatley Hill pit in 1950 and it was part of the role of deputies and senior pit officials that dust suppression measures were kept in proper order. The sprays were in operation where most dust was generated:

where the coal was being cut at the coalface, where it was transferred onto the conveyor belts, and when it was transferred from the conveyor belts into the tubs. Some percussive compressive air drills used to drill stone were fitted with a water feed, but some were not, and the use of electric rotary drills continued without a water feed. In 1954 a fitter was employed in each district underground at Wheatley Hill pit during each shift in order to repair water feeds and related equipment that may break down in order to reduce the amount of time the men were working without water sprays and therefore more susceptible to the coal dust.

Under the NCB's Pneumoconiosis Field Research Project in the 1950s, miners across the coalfield took part in a mass radiography programme in order to determine how many were suffering from pneumoconiosis. In 1959, while attending an appointment at the mobile unit when it visited Wheatley Hill pit yard, my granda was found to have a slight percentage of coal dust in his lungs. When he asked how he could control the condition, he was told 'get out of the pits'. By 1962 his slight percentage had risen to 10 per cent.

As a result of widespread testing, it was found that approximately 5 per cent of miners across the country had some signs of pneumoconiosis.

In 1951 the National Coal Board introduced pensions for workmen retiring at the age of 65 years old, for those obliged to retire before 65 because of ill health and for widows and dependent children. It was a contributory scheme and payments ranged from 10s (50p) per week after sixteen years' service to 30s (£1.50) per week after forty-five years' service, and this would be paid in addition to the state pension at the time of retirement. The Coal Board also contributed to the scheme and Billy Carr saw it as a good plan, signing up in 1951. However, as had always been the case with such things, many miners were slow to support the pension scheme and it was not until 1959 when union membership became compulsory for all new members signing up to work in the coal industry that contributing to the pension scheme was also a requirement.

The symptoms of pneumoconiosis are shortness of breath, tightness in the chest and a chronic cough, all of which my granda suffered with. This led to his resignation from his foreshift overman post in 1963, at which time he became training and safety officer at Wheatley Hill pit. He was never happy in his new role. He loved pit work and the camaraderie that existed there. He was known as a hard taskmaster but also as someone who was firm and fair. The move to an office job was intended to improve his health but it didn't. His health problems continued to intensify, forcing his reluctant early retirement from the coal industry in 1965 at the age of 62.

Once my granda made the decision to finally resign from the pit altogether as a result of his health, there was the question of where he and my grandma would live. For the first time in their lives they would be moving out of colliery-owned accommodation and home ownership looked to be the answer. They didn't consider a council-built house, perhaps advised by their two property-owning sons, neither would they consider a move to Peterlee, where a range of new housing was on offer.

Newhaven, No. 9 Sandwick Terrace, Wheatley Hill.

They were both disappointed to be leaving the Office Street house with its beautiful garden, but even the garden was becoming too much for my granda and eventually they bought a house in Sandwick Terrace, No. 9 or 'Newhaven', as it was named. The only stipulation about where they should live included the need for a garden. Sandwick Terrace, built in the Wingate Lane area of the village during the 1920s, was named after the builder who built the houses, Mr Sandwick from Wingate, and was a street of twenty-six semi-detached houses with a south-facing garden at the back and a small garden at the front. Mr Sandwick retained ownership of some of the houses and the occupants paid him rent, but No. 9 had been sold and used as a hairdressing salon before my grandparents bought it. As a result, while most of the houses had two small rooms downstairs, theirs was one big room that had been used as the salon. Their house also had an attached brick garage built on by the previous owners. However, by this time my granda didn't own a car. My mam and dad bought a car in 1966 and my dad continued to drive my grandparents anywhere they wanted to go.

The task of down-sizing was very difficult. How do you fit the contents of a nine-roomed house into a two-bedroomed modern semi with a box room? My grandma in particular didn't want to be without any of her prized possessions, but realised that she had to make difficult choices. They needed a three-piece suite, and had two to choose from, and after the decorative shelving was removed from their press to avoid the wall lighting in Sandwick Terrace, they had a china cabinet. Together with two rocking chairs, their dining table, dining chairs and matching sideboard, that was all the furniture the living area in their new house would take.

Their bedroom suite, purchased from Sherburn Hill Store at the time of their marriage in 1924, was beautiful. It was dark wood and consisted of a bed, with a feather mattress, double wardrobe, wash stand and dressing table in dark wood. All the pieces just about fit into the front bedroom of the new house. My dad tried to get them to buy a more modern mattress to replace the feathers, and to dispense with the 'turned' sheets, but my grandma wouldn't hear of it. Their bedroom suite from the guest bedroom at Office Street was far too big for the back bedroom in Sandwick Terrace but my grandma was determined to make it fit, rejecting calls to sell it and buy a more modern one. It looked completely out of place in the more modern home, and anyone sleeping there would have great difficulty in accessing the bed, but she wouldn't give in, a situation very reminiscent of her grandma Hannah and her four-poster bed.

The garden was substantial and consisted of a large lawn and flower beds that would be easy to maintain once the initial planting had been carried out. Between them they decided to concentrate on growing roses in the major part of the garden. Their reasoning was that roses are tolerant of a range of soil types and aspects and once planted don't need further planting. My granda ordered a range of roses from an advertisement in the *News of the World* and spent some time making labels for each bush for when they were planted out. The remainder of the growing area was set with vegetables that they would use for themselves and their family.

Despite this necessary relocation into another part of the village, both were happy in their Sandwick Terrace house. My granda became a regular at the New Tavern at the bottom of the street and met up regularly with friends he referred to as 'the lads' to take a stroll around the farms and quarries behind the houses. Unfortunately, he found gardening tasks difficult due to his worsening breathing problems and my grandma worked in the garden, fitting it in alongside her housework. Interestingly, it was my granda who took over the role of shopping and looked forward to his weekly trip to the store, the doorstep deliveries having been abandoned by the mid-1960s.

My grandma was disappointed that the house in Sandwick Terrace didn't have a coal oven and hobs on the fire. The main room (that had been two rooms) had two attractive, modern, 1960s tiled fireplaces, which were not built to accommodate kettles or pans, but she insisted on boiling the kettle on the fire. This was despite having an electric kettle and an electric cooker with oven and hobs. She ignored all calls to stop this dangerous practice and continued to arrange the coals on the fire so that they would accommodate her kettle and ancient pans.

Even after the Second World War, coal was still the dominating employer in the Easington District. Nimmo's Brewery at Castle Eden, Barrass & Walker Mineral Water Factory at Haswell and the Co-operative Dairies at Wingate were the only other significant male employers in the area, and during the early 1960s rumours began to circulate about the possible closure of Wheatley Hill pit. This was intensified in 1962 when neighbouring 125-year-old Wingate pit closed as a result of an exhaustion of economic reserves. This was to become the major concern of east Durham coal miners over the following years.

The closure of Wheatley Hill pit was announced in 1968 when the National Coal Board declared that it had come to the end of its economic workable reserves. A meeting was held at the Welfare Hall in March 1968 to give lodge officials an opportunity of explaining to the men the details of the closure of their 99-year-old pit, and the date was confirmed as 3 May.

There were 650 men employed at the pit and forty were to be retained to take part in salvage work, but the destination of the majority was a major concern, based on the life expectancy of other collieries. Despite the difficult conditions of working at the pit, even at the end of the 1960s, there was a deep regret expressed by workers at having to leave the jobs many of them loved, in the only workplace they had ever known.

The news was devastating to the men who worked at the pit, and being thrust into a situation of change seemed impossible during the early days after the announcement. Pit work was the only work most had ever known and Wheatley Hill pit their only employer, the closure announcement forcing them out of their familiar surroundings. Even just thinking about moving was hard for many to come to terms with. However it was a problem that no one could ignore. Decisions had to be made and in the weeks following the announcement many families had decided which route they were going to take, some taking up the coal board offers of transferring to other pits, which meant increased travelling times and reduced responsibility. Many transferred to other coal areas of the country and others into jobs outside the industry, with early retirement, redundancy and unemployment making up the rest. There was the offer of retraining and while some took up the opportunities on offer, many of the miners were not confident enough to take up any of the training schemes.

The day before the closure was the Easington Divisional Labour Party's May Day parade and ironically Wheatley Hill's turn to host the annual celebration when colliery bands and banners from across the Easington District visited the village. It was a poignant affair as Wheatley Hill band and its banner with a picture of miners' leader Peter Lee was proudly paraded through the village. Local labour MP Emanuel Shinwell marched at the head of the parade and said later, 'It's more like a funeral ceremony than a May Day celebration. May Day has been for many years associated with that great miners' leader, Peter Lee. What is happening today is enough to make him turn in his grave.'

The proud colliery officials marching alongside their banner were lodge secretary Anty Wharrier; the lodge's chairman, Brian Miller, at 24 years old the youngest lodge chairman in the country; treasurer Stephen Wragg and other committee members, including lodge official for over forty years, Edward Cain, who retired from his position in 1956.

The Wheatley Hill brass band was also invited to take part in the cathedral service at the Durham Miners' Gala in 1968 and were delighted to accept the invitation in the last year of their pit.

The annual children's sports day was still held in 1968 despite the pit closure. The event was funded by a 3*d* (3p) a week levy taken from the wages of the miners and there were sufficient funds to cover the cost of the day. This significant day for the children followed the same format as in previous years but it was in the back of everyone's mind that it might be the last.

With the closure of the coal mine in Wheatley Hill came the uncertain future of the Miners' Welfare Park and Hall, which was funded by the miners from money taken weekly from their pay note and where many social events were held. Jack Dormand, education officer for Easington District, held a public meeting in the Welfare Hall at the end of June 1968 and it was decided to form a community association that would take over the running of the hall and its grounds. Wheatley

Hill was the first within the Easington District to be in this situation whereby a facility owned and run by the lodge and funded by its members would now be starved of funding. The Education Committee became involved as it was keen to see the facilities offered at Wheatley Hill Welfare Hall and Park continued for the good of the community. The Education Committee were prepared to grant financial aid up to 75 per cent, and the rest would need to be raised by the new community association, with perhaps a contribution from the parish council. A committee was set up consisting of representatives from all village groups and it became known as Wheatley Hill and District Community Association.

My dad was 40 at the time of the pit closure. A chargehand mechanical fitter with responsibility for carrying out the safety tests on the pit winding engine, but without any other experience of work, he was reluctant to transfer to another pit as he felt that their future was just as uncertain as that of Wheatley Hill. He decided instead to apply for a job at the Whitbread Brewery (formerly Nimmos) at Castle Eden, working as a mechanic in their garage. He was involved in salvage work at Wheatley Hill until September 1968 before commencing his new job at the brewery.

My statutory secondary education ended in 1968 but I opted to stay at school for a further year. The new CSE examinations would give me choices, and I was prepared to work hard in order to prepare for the next stage in my journey through life. I was lucky that I would be supported both at home and at school in order to achieve qualifications and gain confidence that would prepare me. The world I was stepping into was not recognisable from that which my female ancestors who have appeared in my books faced at 16 years old. The choices available to Hannah, illiterate all her life, were limited to following her mother into dressmaking, the alternatives being less attractive, such as cleaning, laundering etc. My great-grandmother, Susan, was able to read and write and by 1873 she too chose the family business of dressmaking. By 1917 my grandma, Bella, had more choices, but they continued to be related to service in some way. The dressmaking route wasn't available to her as a result of the ready-to-wear market being well-developed by that time. She worked on a farm for a short time before going to 'place' at Redcar as a maid of all work in a private school, returning to Ludworth to work for Mr White, the schoolmaster, as his housekeeper, until her marriage.

The next in line of succession was my dad, but I can't compare him as, being a man, his choices in 1942 would mostly be related to pit work, and as I have mentioned earlier, even taking this route, without a good education, could still lead to further and higher education and training depending on individual determination and ambition.

When I left Wheatley Hill Girls School, aged 16, it would be with qualifications that would guarantee me a job as an office junior or a place at one of the local technical colleges to gain further qualifications so that I could enter the jobs market at a higher level, aged 18. I had choices that weren't available to previous generations of my family and despite my lack of a grammar school education I had a determination inherited from those females who had gone before me, and determination and ambition inherited from my mother. As a result of my slow start to educational achievement, I quickly realised that education could be for life and with hard work and commitment I could continue my learning journey. And I did.

END WORDS

Bella never forgot where she came from. For the whole of her 95 years, she continued to speak in glowing terms of the village she was born in that held such obviously happy memories for her, despite its appalling housing conditions and lack of basic amenities. Always describing it as 'a lovely little village', her memories were based on people and not on places. She valued the neighbours who were like family, the community spirit and the fact that, being such a small village, everyone was known to everyone else. She loved being part of the close-knit community and was devastated when she had to leave it.

Being brought up in a close and happy family where love and support were unconditional, these are the features that my grandma carried with her throughout her life, always putting her family first and valuing time spent with them above everything else. This was often at the expense of invitations from friends and neighbours who were only too happy to include her in outings etc. over the years, but she always declined. This may have made her appear standoffish to some, but she certainly wasn't. The reasons for her reluctance to become involved were straightforward to her; it was in case a member of her family needed her on that particular day. So many lost opportunities to socialise and make her own social networks but never regretted in the least by my grandma.

Despite my grandma's closeness to her neighbours over the years, she never referred to any of them by their given names. She always called them by their title, 'Mrs' or 'Mr' etc. This was not connected to how little or well she knew them; this was how she had been brought up and she continued in this respectful manner throughout her life.

Throughout this series of books, I have been able to place on the public record the human activity of a family that had never made it before, and without my books, probably never would. It's always amazing to hear the memories that are passed on through families, some seemingly trivial and of no value, such as my grandma being very proud of her grandma Hannah's three-tier jam tart. We wonder why that memory was valued and deemed important enough to pass on, and why it took precedence over other memories, but it did and so it is with the memories I have presented in this book. We can only assume that it adds to the richness of the family story.

My family is an ordinary coal mining family from east Durham, no better or worse than anyone else's family, just a family where one person has taken the time to tell their story, and in terms of mining history, women's history and social history I think that's important. My hope is that readers will have been motivated by the story to carry out their own family history research or find out more information about some of the issues I've mentioned for themselves and realise that it can be done. If either of these things happen, then I think my books have been successful.

Writing myself into the narrative has been very difficult and I have been beset with continuous feelings of self-doubt and insecurity at putting my own story on the public record, but I want readers to know that I am writing from a good place, with only the best intentions. The story of seemingly unimportant people can provide insights into our history that would otherwise go unnoticed and unremarked on, and it is from these family stories that we are likely to find something that challenges the views of eminent historians.

The old proverb 'A Woman's Place is in the Home' is a notion that has probably been expressed by hundreds of people over many years, but fully supported by women married to coal miners during the nineteenth and much of the twentieth century. It was from these ideals that my female relatives, as a result of training received from their mothers, learned how to run a home and look after a family and in the case of my grandma and many women like her, it was something she supported for the whole of her life. She understood the need to move when her husband's job demanded it but no doubt the last move from Office Street to Sandwick Terrace was the most difficult, for the first time in her life, moving away from the shadow of the pit that had dominated her life. However, both she and my granda were happy in Sandwick Terrace and it was where they lived out the rest of their days.

BIBLIOGRAPHY

Books and Articles

Beynn, H. & Austrin, T., *Masters and Servants* (London: Rivers Oram Press, 1994)

Bulmer, M. (ed), *Mining & Social Change* (Croom Helm, 1978)

Carr, Griselda, *Pit Women: Coal Communities in Northern England in the Early Twentieth Century* (Merlin Press, 2001)

Easington District Rural Council, *Farewell Squalor* (Easington Rural District Council, 1946)

Garside, W., *The Durham Miners 1919–1960* (George Allen & Unwin Ltd, 1971)

Halme, H., *Write Your Story* (Newhurst Press, 2017)

Knayston, D., *Austerity Britain 1945–1957* (Bloomsbury, 2007)

Moyes, W.A., *Mostly Mining* (Frank Graham, NUT, 1969)

Office for National Statistics, *New Earnings Survey* (NES) time-series of gross weekly earnings from 1938 to 2017

Philipson, G., *Aycliffe and Peterlee New Towns 1946–1988* (Publications for Companies, 1988)

Rentzenbrink, C., *Write it All Down* (Bluebird, 2022)

Temple, D., *The Big Meeting – a History of the Durham Miners Gala* (TUPS Books in Association with the DMA, 2011)

Thompson, E.P., *The History of William Morris* (Parthenon Books, 1955)

Turnbull, L., *Hidden Treasures* (North of England Institute of Mining and Mechanical Engineers in association with the Newcastle Centre of the Stephenson Locomotive Society, 2021)

Wheatley Hill History Club, *The Employees & Residents of Thornley, Ludworth and Wheatley Hill: Their Contribution to the Second World War* (Wheatley Hill History Club, 2009)

Wheatley Hill History Club, *The National Coal Board, Owners of Thornley, Ludworth and Wheatley Hill Collieries 1947–1955* (Wheatley Hill History Club, 2006)

Wheatley Hill History Club, *The National Coal Board, Owners of Thornley, Ludworth and Wheatley Hill Collieries 1956–1976* (Wheatley Hill History Club, 2008)

Wheatley Hill History Club Newsletter (Vol. 12 Issue 2), https://wheatley-hill.org.uk, April 2010

Unpublished

Carr, W.H., An Unpublished Holiday Diary, 1948–1981

Carr, W.H., Draft Health Questionnaire in respect of Pneumoconiosis, 1962

Tunney, H. & T., At the Coalface of the Labour Party: Hubert Tunney, Durham Miner (1890–1958) (in very long unpublished manuscript in possession of Wheatley Hill History Club, 2023, https://wheatley-hill.org.uk)

Wheatley Hill School Registers (1948–65)

Newspapers

The Daily Express, 29 November 1961, *in Aycliffe and Peterlee New Towns 1946–1988*, p.145

The Durham Chronicle, online at Find My Past

The Durham County Advertiser, online at Find My Past

Recordings
Carr, G., A Life Interview (1995)
Carr, I.J., A Life Interview (1995)

Websites
https://en.wikipedia.org/wiki/Doggarts
https://jnnp.bmj.com
www.educationengland.org.uk/history/chapter08